Big Day in the Neighborhood

CONTENTS

NATIONAL GEOGRAPHIC  Hampton-Brown

School Publishing

Words with Short a

Look at each picture. Read the words.

a

Example:

c**a**p

p**a**n

c**a**t

v**a**n

h**a**t

m**a**n

s**a**x

Key Words

Look at the picture. Read the sentences.

Jan Helps Dad

1. It is a big **day** for Dad at the stand.
2. **There** is a lot to **do**.
3. **What** can Jan do to **help** Dad?
4. Jan can sit **by** Rags.
5. **Then** **people** can stop and shop.

Will Jan have to sit by Rags all day?

Phonics Games

NGReach.com

3

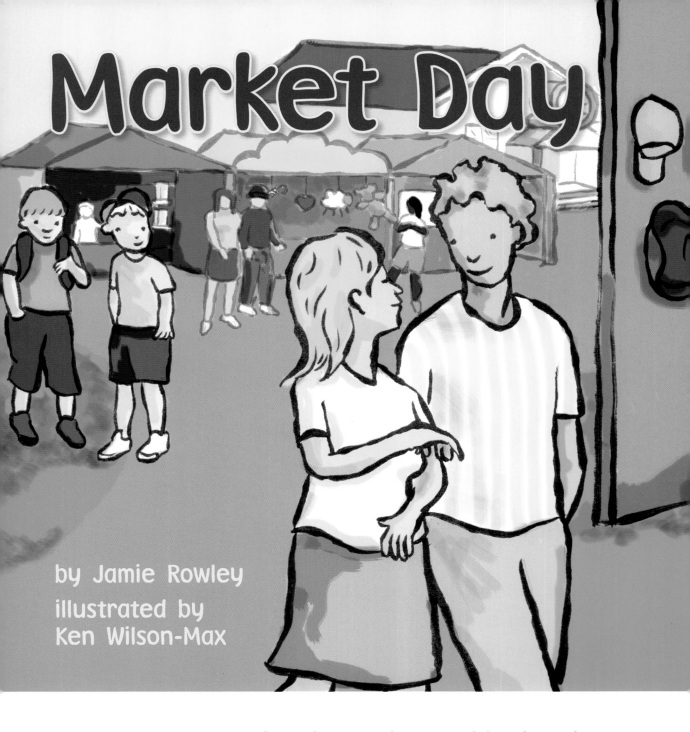

Market Day

by Jamie Rowley

illustrated by
Ken Wilson-Max

It is market day in the neighborhood.
You can see and do a lot at the market!

My dad has a stand there. He sells hats
and caps. His pal Cam has pots and pans.

Max has bags and sacks.

Pat has jam. Pat has cans of ham, too.
Pat sells jam and ham as people go by.

I can help Dad at the stand.

mat

My Lab, Sam, can help, too. Sam sits
on a mat. Sam wags as people go by.
People pat Sam and then get a cap.

I see my pals at the market. My
pal Dan and his dad are there. Dan
pats Sam.

His dad gets a cap.

At 6, the hats and caps go in the van.
Sam and I help Dad.

I sit in the van. Sam naps on my lap.

We had a fun day! What would you get at the market? ❖

Words with Short a

Read these words.

hat	him	man	up	van
tag	hit	Lab	bat	bag

Find the words with short **a**.
Use letters to build them.

h   a   t

Choose words from the box above
to tell your partner about the picture.

The man has
a Lab .

Learn Phonics

Words with Short i

Look at each picture. Read the words.

i

Example:

p**i**n

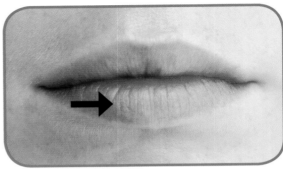

l**i**p

b**i**n

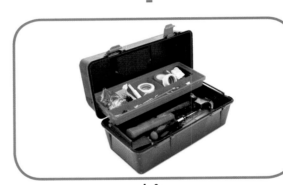

k**i**t

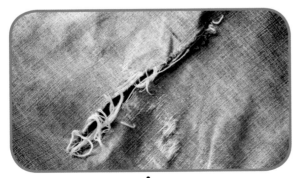

r**i**p

k**i**d

Key Words

Look at the pictures.
Read the sentences.

High Frequency Words

by
day
do
help
people
then
there
what

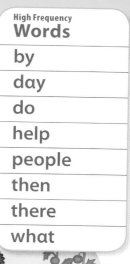

People Can Help

1. **What** can we **do** to **help**?
2. **People** can dig.
3. **Then** people can mix.
4. **There** are jobs kids can do.
5. **Day** **by** day the plants get big!

What will the kids do to help?

Phonics Games

NGReach.com

17

A Neighborhood Garden

by Jamie Rowley

That land is bare. What can go in there?

A garden can go in that land. A
neighborhood garden can go there.

People plan and talk. What will
we do? What will we plant?

We will dig. We will plant. If people help, then it will go fast.

People help in the garden. People dig and plant. People help tend the plants.

bin

plant in pot

People fix a bin. Plants begin
in pots and then go in big bins
in the garden.

What can kids do to help? Kids
can do a lot! Kids can dig and plant.
Kids can pick up trash.

Kids can care for the plants day by
day. This helps little plants get big.

Kids help in big and little gardens.
This big garden has vegetables.

This little garden has vegetables.

This little garden has big, big flowers! ❖

Words with Short i

Read these words.

sip	sit	hat	dig	man
mix	fix	quit	cat	rip

Find the words with short **i**.
Use letters to build them.

s   i   p

Talk Together

Choose words from the box
above to tell your partner
about the pictures.

People dig and mix.

Help Tim

It is Market day. Help Tim find 5 things at the market. Take turns with a partner. Put a marker on each thing.

1. Go to the stand that has hats. Find a hat with a tan band.
2. Go to the stand with kits. Then find a tan kit.
3. There are bags and a Lab at this stand. Find a big bag by the Lab.
4. What stand has a man with pans? Find a pan's lid at this stand.
5. Go to a stand with bats. Find a bat.

Acknowledgments

Grateful acknowledgment is given to the authors, artists, photographers, museums, publishers, and agents for permission to reprint copyrighted material. Every effort has been made to secure the appropriate permission. If any omissions have been made or if corrections are required, please contact the Publisher.

Photographic Credits

CVR Alvaro Leiva/age fotostock/Photolibrary. **2** (bl) Timothy Large/Shutterstock. (br) Knud Nielsen/Shutterstock. (cl) Pawel Strykowski/Shutterstock. (tc) R. Mackay Photography/Shutterstock. (tl) Mackey Creations/Shutterstock. **3** Liz Garza Williams/Hampton-Brown/National Geographic School Publishing. **7** (bg) Angelo Gilardelli/Shutterstock. **15** Liz Garza Williams/Hampton-Brown/National Geographic School Publishing. **16** (bcr) Ahmad Hamoudah/iStockphoto. (bl) Karen Keczmerski/iStockphoto. (br) Nina Shannon/iStockphoto. (cl) SasPartout/Shutterstock. (tcr) Anthony Harris/Shutterstock. (tl) Image Club. **17** Liz Garza Williams/Hampton-Brown/National Geographic School Publishing. **18** (inset) Stacy Barnett/Shutterstock. **18-19** (bg) Richard Levine/Alamy Images. **20** Michael Newman/PhotoEdit. **21** Rowan Isaac/Garden Picture Library/Photolibrary. **22-23** (l) Amy Sussman/Corbis. **23** (b) Syracuse Newspapers/Li-Hau Lan/The Image Works, Inc. (t) Jim West/The Image Works, Inc. **24** Jupiterimages/Getty Images. **25** David Young-Wolff/PhotoEdit. **26-27** (l) Ariel Skelley/Blend Images/age fotostock. **27** Garden Pix LTD/Photolibrary. **28** Juice Images/Photolibrary. **29** Liz Garza Williams/Hampton-Brown/National Geographic School Publishing.

Illustrator Credits

3, 15, 17, 29 Constanza Basaluzzo; **4-14** Ken Max-Wilson; **30-31** Mattia Cerato

The National Geographic Society

John M. Fahey, Jr., President & Chief Executive Officer
Gilbert M. Grosvenor, Chairman of the Board

National Geographic School Publishing
Hampton-Brown
www.NGSP.com

Printed in the USA.
Quad Graphics, Leominster, MA

ISBN:978-0-7362-8056-3

18 19
10 9 8 7 6

kaffe knits again

kaffe knits again

photographed by **sheila rock** at Charleston

24 original designs updated for today's knitters by **kaffe fassett**

POTTER
CRAFT

This book is dedicated to the artists who created Charleston House and to those who so lovingly preserve it.

Published in the United States by Potter Craft, an imprint of the Crown Publishing Group, a division of Random House, Inc., New York.
www.clarksonpotter.com
www.pottercraft.com

POTTER CRAFT and CLARKSON N. POTTER are trademarks, and POTTER and colophon are registered trademarks of Random House, Inc.

Library of Congress Cataloging-in-Publication Data

Fassett, Kaffe.
  Kaffe knits again : 24 original designs updated for today's knitters / by Kaffe Fassett ; photographed by Sheila Rock at Charleston.
     p. cm.
  ISBN-13: 978-0-307-39538-2 (hardcover) 1. Knitting—Patterns. I. Title.
  TT820.F3454 2007
  746.43'2041—dc22

                            2007021603

Printed in Singapore

Editor Sally Harding
Designer Christine Wood
Location Photography Sheila Rock
Flat-shot Photography John Heseltine
Stylist Elaine Briggs
Charts Sally Harding
Pattern writer Sue Whiting
Pattern checker Stella Smith

Associate publisher Susan Berry

10 9 8 7 6 5 4 3 2 1

First Edition

contents

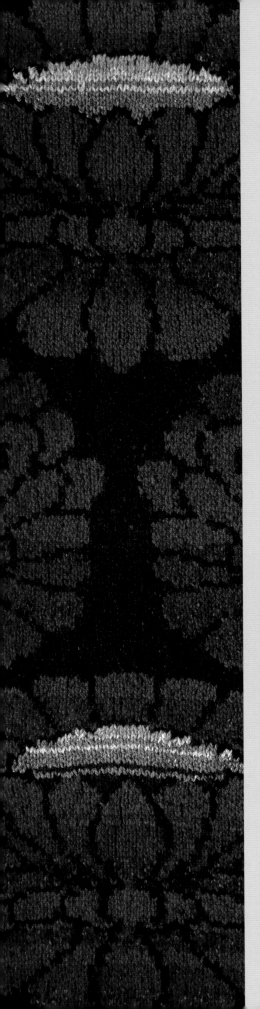

introduction

There is a myth in the knitting community that color knitting is very complicated and only the most experienced knitters can master it, so a lot of colorwork knits are only glanced at and then passed over for simpler-looking fare. Occasionally, though, a first-time knitter who hasn't been warned will try one of my bold, patterned knits and carry it off with great aplomb—proving that they are not as scary as they appear!

I pour my heart and soul into my designs, so I am disappointed when they are dismissed by even experienced knitters as too difficult to attempt. With this book I am giving all nervous knitters the opportunity to try out color knitting. Using current Rowan yarns, I've reinterpreted some of my favorite patterns from years past that deserve a second chance.

Many of the patterns have been transformed from coats and sweaters into easier projects like scarves, throws, shawls, or cushions. Working simple knitted squares, strips, or rectangles is an excellent way to break into patterned knitting; it allows you to concentrate on the color knitting without having to cope with increases or decreases. There are several simple two-color-a-row designs as well as more challenging fare.

I hope you will experience, as I do, the deep pleasure of watching a colored pattern unfold as you knit from row to row. If it grabs you as it does me, you will discover that working one-color garments is quite monotonous by comparison.

It was fun for me to revisit some of my designs and give them a different personality by changing the color palettes. You will see from the variety of items in this book that you can translate any of my motifs into simple cushion, scarf, or throw shapes and even work them on larger needles, using the yarn doubled. A small tidy motif in a fine yarn becomes delightfully big and blousy when knitted in a chunky weight on large needles—like the Big Flower Throw on pages 16 and 17.

After the joy of playing with new colors and shapes, my next task was to find the location to show off these new knits. I wanted sympathetic colors and textures where my patterns and colors would feel at home and look their best. Casting my mind over the many possible places I'd seen in my travels up and down the British Isles, it struck me that no place has as much atmosphere and delicious color as Charleston House in Sussex. It is filled with beautiful handmade surfaces lovingly created by the artists that made it their home in the early 1900s: Duncan Grant, Vanessa Bell, Dora Carrington, and many others painted murals, furniture, and floors in the house, and created needlepoints, rugs, lamps, and pottery for it as well. Most of the objects in the house have a painterly surface in a wonderful, sophisticated palette.

When the models took up their positions in these rooms wearing my garments, they became figures in a tapestry. My cushions and throws look so at home that you would think they were made specially for the place. All of us on the book team were amazed by the rightness of my designs nestled in the ambience of Charleston.

—Kaffe Fassett

gallery of designs

left: **Crisscross** page 13—*see pages 116–119 for instructions*
right: **Jack's Back** page 13—*see pages 120–122 for instructions*

Houses Bag page 14
see pages 92–93 for instructions

Houses page 15
see pages 106–109 for instructions

Big Flower Throw
pages 16–17
see pages 110–113 for instructions

Crosspatch page 19
see pages 88–91 for instructions

Gridlock Throw pages 20–21
see pages 126–129 for instructions

Stepped Flowers Stole
page 22
see pages 102–105 for instructions

Moody Blues Cushion
page 24
see pages 72–73 for instructions

Domino Cushion page 25
see pages 78–79 for instructions

Polka Dots page 26
see pages 64–68 for instructions

Foolish Virgins Scarf
pages 28–29
see pages 132–135 for instructions

Reflections pages 30–31
see pages 56–59 for instructions

Brocade Throw pages 32–33
see pages 80–83 for instructions

Caterpillar Stripes
pages 34–35—*see pages
114–115 for instructions*

Tumbling Blocks page 37
*see pages 98–101 for
instructions*

Cheviot Gardens
pages 38–39
see pages 74–77 for instructions

Mirage page 40
see pages 94–97 for instructions

Dark Daisy pages 42–43
see pages 60–63 for instructions

Squiggle Stripe
pages 44–45
see pages 84–87 for instructions

Tulips pages 46–47
*see pages 123–125 for
instructions*

Chinese Lanterns page 49
see pages 69–71 for instructions

Puzzle pages 50–51
*see pages 136–140 for
instructions*

Gridlock Cushion
pages 52–53—*see pages
130–131 for instructions*

near right: **Crisscross**

Inspired by bold African textiles, the monochromatic grays and blacks of this men's crewneck make it very versatile, but it would be easy to substitute soft colors if preferred. *See pages 116–119 for instructions.*

far right: **Jack's Back**

The shades chosen for this V-neck are the soft natural hues of a stony beach. The design uses only two colors per row, making it easy to knit. *See pages 120–122 for instructions. (See page 24 for the Moody Blues Cushion on the chair.)*

left: Houses Bag
The rows of windows in the knitted house on this bag create a strongly graphic pattern set off well by the checked borders. *See pages 92–93 for instructions.*

above: Houses
This version of my popular Houses sleeveless V-neck uses particularly appealing color combinations. *See pages 106–109 for instructions.*

above and far right: **Big Flower Throw**
This bold, dynamic design uses only two
colors per row for most of the charted
pattern and is worked on large needles, so
it is quick to knit for its size. Use it as a throw
or a chair cover. *See pages 110–113
for instructions. (See pages 30–31 for the
Reflections vest, and page 15 for the Houses
sleeveless V-neck.)*

right: **Crosspatch**

The subtle colors at Charleston House are the perfect backdrop for my design. The outlined crosses of this sleeveless V-neck give it a delicate, timeless quality, and the updated coloring makes it suitable for men and women. *See pages 88–91 for instructions.*

left and above: **Gridlock Throw**

The orginal geometric pattern for this throw was taken from an ancient carpet. This new coloring is worked with two strands of a fine wool yarn held together. *See pages 126–129 for instructions.*

far left: **Stepped Flowers Stole**
The fresco palette on this shawl melts and
harmonizes superbly with the soft colors of
the studio at Charleston. The geometric pattern
is easy to memorize, which makes it an
enjoyable knitting project. *See pages
102–105 for instructions.*

left: **Moody Blues Cushion**
Adapted from what was originally a sweater design, this cushion in soft, warm tones is perfectly at home on an old chair in Vanessa Bell's studio at Charleston. *See pages 72–73 for instructions.*

right: **Domino Cushion**
The strong dots-on-squares geometry in this design makes it look a little like a jockey's colorful uniform. As a cushion, it makes a good punctuation in any room. *See pages 78–79 for instructions.*

left: **Polka Dots**

Each of the vertical stripes on this cotton cardigan uses only two colors per row, so it is one of the easiest designs in the book to knit. The cool palette is quite feminine, but if you prefer, you could use violet for the dots and dark navy, brown, and teal for the background stripes. *See pages 64–68 for instructions.*

right: **Foolish Virgins Scarf**

This scarf is an exciting sampler of many of my pattern motifs. You could take any one of the seven charted patterns and repeat it to make a variation of this scarf, or use it for a cushion cover, shawl, or throw. *See pages 132–135 for instructions.*

left and above: **Reflections**

With only two colors per row, this cotton women's (or men's) vest would make a great first
Kaffe Fassett pattern for a beginner knitter. *See pages 56–59 for instructions.*

above and right: **Brocade Throw**

Old brocades inspired the bold patterns on this cotton throw. The change of color and pattern

give the illusion of a patchwork of strips of different fabrics. *See pages 80–83 for instructions.*

left and right: **Caterpillar Stripes**

If you want to knit my designs without having to master colorwork knitting, this is the sweater for you. The rich tones of this sweater make the simple stripe design as lush as my more complex patterns. *See pages 114–115 for instructions.*

right: **Tumbling Blocks**

Revisited many times in my work, the classic tumbling blocks design can be found on ancient Peruvian baskets and Roman floors. As complex as it might first appear, the pattern it is easy to memorize after you have knitted a couple of repeats. Men seem to like the architectural strength of the block shapes. *See pages 98–101 for instructions.*

left and far right:
Cheviot Gardens
Inspired by French wallpaper, the
small-scale motifs and gently
changing colors of this cotton
cardigan create a dappled, rippling
effect. The simple two-color-a-row
repeats are easy to memorize.
See pages 74–77 for instructions.

left: **Mirage**

Although the format of the pattern on this crewneck is from an old kilim, it took on the heat haze of a mirage in a desert since I created it while traveling long, hot roads in India. This is a challenging knit and won't go terribly fast, but I hope you will enjoy the journey through its rich landscape.
See pages 94–97 for instructions.

left and above: **Dark Daisy**

There is a quiet drama to the scale of the dark daisies on this long cotton tunic. For a change of mood, you could knit maroon daisies on a purple background, or use pastel colors. *See pages 60–63 for instructions.*

above and right: **Squiggle Stripe**

The series of little squiggles break up the very close tones of the striped ground on this cotton vest. It creates almost a marble effect. *See pages 84–87 for instructions.*

left and right: **Tulips**

The tulips and sinuous leaves on this cotton sweater echo the lively movement seen in lush floral fabric prints. A pale blue or pink background color would be perfect for a more feminine look. *See pages 123–125 for instructions.*

right: **Chinese Lanterns**

For a different palette on this cotton cardigan, try dramatic orange to dark red lantern motifs on a black background. If you don't like the idea of changing the colors within the lantern motifs, you could use a space-dyed yarn instead. *See pages 69–71 for instructions.*

above and right: **Puzzle**

I first spotted the puzzle design used on this wool cardigan in an old art deco hotel in America. It was a black and white tile formation on a bathroom floor—a seemingly unlikely place to find a knitting design source! *See pages 136–140 for instructions.*

left and right: **Gridlock Cushion**
Worked with a single strand of a fine
yarn, this design produces a more
delicate rendition of the gridlock format
also used for the throw on pages
20 and 21. *See pages 130–131
for instructions.*

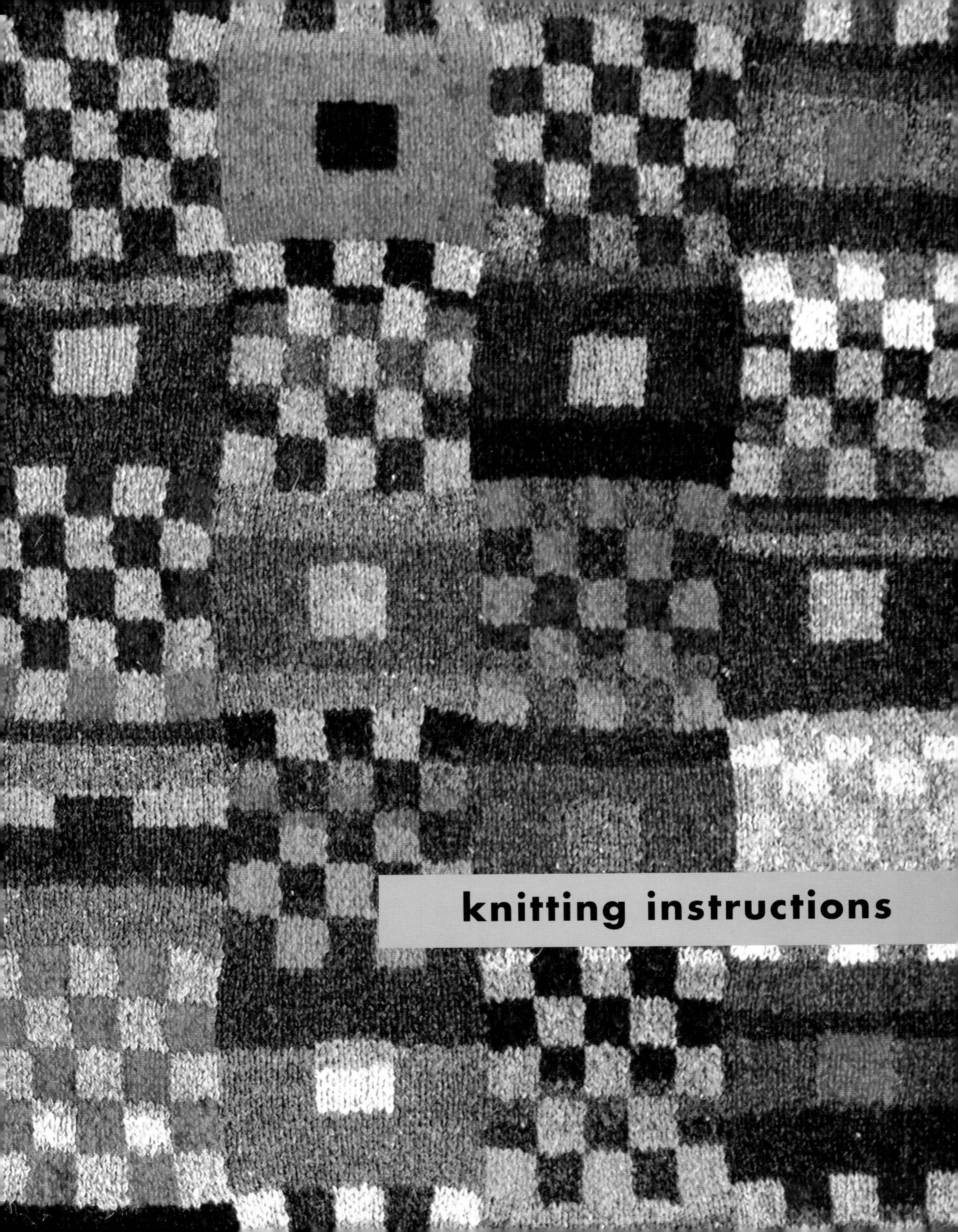

knitting instructions

reflections

sizes and measurements

To fit bust/chest	36–38	40–42	44	in
	91–97	102–107	112	cm

Finished knitted measurements

Around bust/chest	45	47	49	in
	114	119	124	cm
Length to shoulder	22	22	22	in
	56	56	56	cm

yarn

Rowan *Cotton Glace* (50g/1¾oz per ball) as foll:

A	Blood Orange 445	2	2	2	balls
B	Hyacinth 787	2	2	2	balls
C	Poppy 741	1	1	1	ball
D	Ivy 812	2	2	2	balls
E	Chocolate 816	1	2	2	balls
F	Excite 815	1	2	2	balls
G	Mystic 808	1	2	2	balls
H	Hot Lips 818	1	1	2	balls
J	Dijon 739	1	1	1	ball
L	Black 727	3	3	3	balls
M	Nightshade 746	1	1	2	balls

needles

Pair of size 2 (2.75mm) knitting needles
Pair of size 3 (3.25mm) knitting needles, *or size to obtain correct gauge*
Size 2 (2.75mm) circular knitting needle, 32in/80cm long

extras

5 buttons

gauge

25 sts and 32 rows to 4in/10cm measured over St st chart pattern using size 3 (3.25mm) needles. *Note: To save time, take time to check gauge.*

special chart note

When reading St st chart, read all odd-numbered RS (knit) rows from right to left and all even-numbered WS (purl) rows from left to right. Use the Fair Isle technique, weaving color not in use into back of work.
To avoid weaving in lots of loose ends when knitting is complete, weave in ends on WS of knitting when joining in and cutting off yarns.

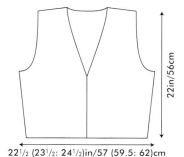

22in/56cm

22½ (23½: 24½)in/57 (59.5: 62)cm

back

Using size 2 (2.75mm) needles and yarn L, cast on 108 (114: 120) sts.
Beg with a K row, work 10 rows in St st.
Next row (RS) P to end, to form fold line.
Next row (inc row) P7 (10: 3), [M1, P5 (5: 6)] 19 times, M1, P6 (9: 3). 128 (134: 140) sts.
Change to size 3 (3.25mm) needles.
Set St st chart patt (see pages 58 and 59) on next 2 rows as foll:
Chart row 1 (RS) K across row, working 0 (0: 1)B, 5 (8: 10)A,

[1B, 10A] twice, 1B, 11A, [1B, 10A] 4 times, 1B, 11A, [1B, 10A] 3 times, 0 (1:1)B, 0 (2: 5)A.

Chart row 2 P across row, working 0 (1: 4)A, 0 (2: 2)B, 9A, 3B, 8A, 3B, [9A, 2B] 3 times, 9A, 3B, 8A, 3B, [9A, 2B] 3 times, 9A, 3B, 4 (7: 8)A, 0 (0: 2)B.

Cont in St st chart patt as set until chart row 96 has been completed *and at the same time* inc 1 st at each end of chart row 17 and every foll 6th row until there are 142 (148: 154) sts, ending with a WS row.

Shape armholes

Keeping chart patt correct throughout, bind off 5 (6: 7) sts at beg of next 2 rows.

Bind off 3 (4: 5) sts at beg of next 2 rows.

Dec 1 st at each end of next 5 rows, 3 foll alt rows, then 3 foll 4th rows. 104 (106: 108) sts.

Work even until chart row 180 has been completed, ending with a WS row.

Shape shoulders and back neck

Bind off 5 sts at beg of next 6 rows.

Next row (RS) Bind off 5 sts, work in patt until there are 20 (21: 22) sts on right needle, then turn, leaving rem sts on a holder.

Cont on these 20 (21: 22) sts only for right side of neck.

Bind off 4 sts at beg of next row.

Bind off 5 sts at beg of next row.

Bind off 2 sts at beg of next row.

Bind off 5 sts at beg of next row.

Work even for 1 row.

Bind off rem 4 (5: 6) sts.

With RS facing, rejoin yarn to rem sts and bind off center 24 sts, then work in patt to end.

Complete to match first side, reversing shapings.

left front

Using size 2 (2.75mm) needles and yarn L, cast on 54 (57: 60) sts.

Beg with a K row, work 10 rows in St st.

Next row (RS) P to end, to form fold line.

Next row (inc row) P5 (6: 3), [M1, P5 (5: 6)] 9 times, M1, P4 (6: 3). 64 (67: 70) sts.

Change to size 3 (3.25mm) needles.

Beg with chart row 1, work in patt foll chart between markers for left front until chart row 90 has been completed *and at the same time* inc 1 st at beg of chart row 17 and every foll 6th row until there are 71 (74: 77) sts, ending with a WS row.

Shape front neck and armhole

Keeping chart patt correct throughout, dec 1 st at neck edge on next row and every foll 5th row until there are 34 (35: 36) sts *and at the same time* when chart row 96 has been completed, shape armhole as for back, ending with a WS row.

Shape shoulder

Bind off 5 sts at beg of next row and 5 foll alt rows.

Bind off rem 4 (5: 6) sts.

right front

Work as for left front, foll chart between markers for right front and reversing shapings.

to finish

Block pieces as explained on page 141.

Sew both shoulder seams, using backstitch.

Button band

With RS facing and using size 2 (2.75mm) circular needle, pick up and knit sts up right front, across back neck, and down left front in colors as foll:

Starting at hemline fold on right front and using yarn E, pick up and knit 11 sts along row ends of first band of patt (to chart row 15); using yarn J, pick up and knit 15 sts along 2nd band; using yarn B, 13 sts along 3rd band; using yarn A, 14 sts along 4th band; using yarn H, 14 sts along 5th band; using yarn L, 12 sts along 6th band; using yarn B, 13 sts along 7th band; using yarn E, 11 sts along 8th band; using yarn J, 15 sts along 9th band; using yarn B, 13 sts along 10th band; using yarn A, 14 sts along 11th band, ending at shoulder seam**; then pick up and knit 40 sts in total across back neck, using yarn H for first 14 sts, yarn L for center 12 sts, yarn H for last 14 sts, and ending at shoulder seam; cont down left front edge working colors in reverse from **. 330 sts.

Keeping colors as set, work band as foll:

Row 1 (WS) P to end.

Row 2 K to end.

Row 3 (buttonhole row) (WS) P2, [P2tog, yo twice, P2tog tbl, P11] 4 times, P2tog, yo twice, P2tog tbl, P1.

Row 4 K to end.

Cut off all yarns.

Using yarn L only, cont as foll:

Row 5 (WS) P to end.

Row 6 P to end, to form fold line.

Beg with a P row, work 5 rows more in St st, working buttonholes on 3rd of these rows (a WS row) to correspond with those made previously.

Bind off loosely.

Fold band to WS along fold line and slip stitch in place.

Armhole edgings

With RS facing and using size 2 (2.75mm) needles and yarn L, pick up and knit 140 sts evenly around armhole edge.

Row 1 (WS) P to end.

Row 2 K to end.

Row 3 K to end, to form fold line.

Beg with a K row, work 2 rows in St st.

Bind off very loosely.

Sew side seams.

Fold armhole edgings and lower hem to WS along fold lines and slip stitch in place.

Press seams lightly on WS, following instructions on yarn label.

Sew on buttons to correspond with buttonholes.

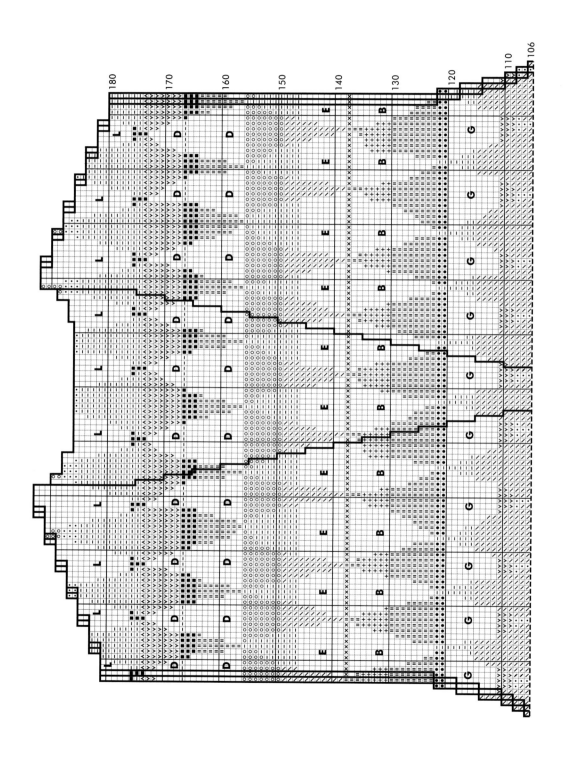

KEY

	A	B	C	D	E	F	G	H	J	L	M
=	•	+	✕	>	ꞁ	○	■	<	●	╱

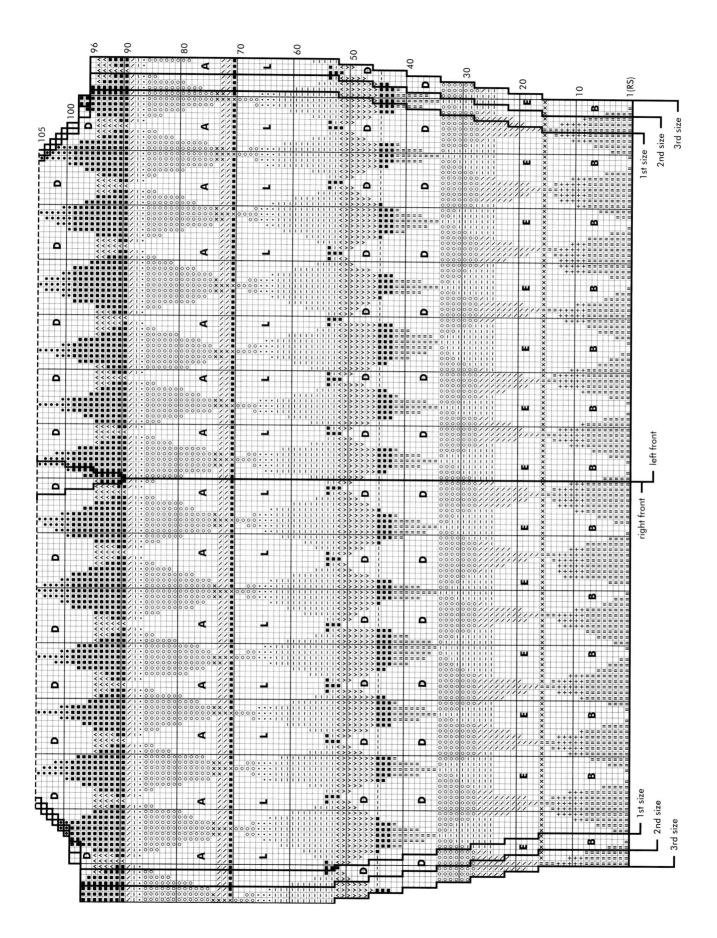

dark daisy

sizes and measurements

To fit bust	34–36	38–40	in
	86–91	97–102	cm

Finished knitted measurements

Around bust	42	44	in
	106	112	cm
Length to shoulder	28	29	in
	71	73.5	cm
Sleeve seam	18¼	18¼	in
	45.5	45.5	cm

yarn

Rowan *Handknit Cotton* (50g/1¾oz per ball) as foll:

A	Black 252	7	7	balls
B	Turkish Plum *277*	12	12	balls
C	Spanish Red *307*	1	1	ball
D	Decadent *314*	1	1	ball
F	Double Chocolate *315*	1	1	ball

needles

Pair of size 3 (3.25mm) knitting needles
Pair of size 6 (4mm) knitting needles, *or size to obtain correct gauge*

gauge

20 sts and 28 rows to 4in/10cm measured over St st chart pattern using size 6 (4mm) needles. *Note: To save time, take time to check gauge.*

special chart note

When reading St st chart, read all odd-numbered RS (knit) rows from right to left and all even-numbered WS (purl) rows from left to right. Use the intarsia technique, using a separate length of yarn for each area of color and twisting yarns together on WS where they meet to avoid holes. (Do NOT carry background color (A) across row, but use a separate length of yarn for each area as for other colors.) To avoid weaving in lots of loose ends when knitting is complete, weave in ends on WS of knitting when joining in and cutting off yarns.

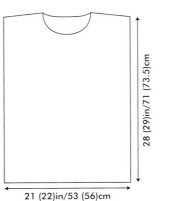

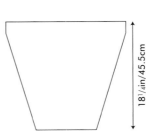

28 (29)in/71 (73.5)cm

21 (22)in/53 (56)cm

18¼in/45.5cm

back

Using size 3 (3.25mm) needles and yarn A, cast on 106 (112) sts.
Work 6 rows in garter st (K every row), ending with a WS row.
Change to size 6 (4mm) needles.
Set St st chart patt (see pages 62 and 63) on next 2 rows as foll:
Chart row 1 (RS) K across row, working 0 (2)B, 6 (7)A, 7B, 31A, 10B, 7A, 7B, 35A, 3 (6)B.
Chart row 2 P across row, working 4 (7)B, 33A, 9B, 5A, 12B, 29A, 9B, 5 (6)A, 0 (2)B.
Cont in St st chart patt as set until chart row 192 (200) has been completed, ending with a WS row.

Shape shoulders and back neck

Next row (RS) Bind off 11 (12) sts, work in patt until there are 28 (30) sts on right needle, then turn, leaving rem sts on a holder.
Cont on these 28 (30) sts only for right side of neck.
Keeping chart patt correct throughout, bind off 4 sts at beg of next row.
Next row (RS) Bind off 11 (12) sts, work in patt to last 2 sts, K2tog.
Next row P2tog, work in patt to end.
Bind off rem 11 (12) sts.
With RS facing, rejoin yarn to rem sts and bind off center 28 sts, then work in patt to end.
Complete to match first side, reversing shapings.

front

Work as for back until chart row 172 (180) has been completed, ending with a WS row.

Divide for neck

Next row (RS) Work 43 (46) sts in patt, then turn, leaving rem sts on a holder.
Cont on these 43 (46) sts only for left side of neck.
Keeping chart patt correct throughout, dec 1 st at neck edge on next 6 rows and 4 foll alt rows. 33 (36) sts.
Work even until front matches back to shoulder shaping, ending with a WS row.

Shape left shoulder

Bind off 11 (12) sts at beg of next row and foll alt row.
Work even for 1 row.
Bind off rem 11 (12) sts.
With RS facing, rejoin yarn to rem sts and bind off center 20 sts, then work in patt to end. 43 (46) sts.
Complete to match first side, reversing shapings.

sleeves (make 2)

Using size 3 (3.25mm) needles and yarn A, cast on 50 sts.
Work 6 rows in garter st, ending with a WS row.
Change to size 6 (4mm) needles.
Beg with chart row 1, work in chart patt between markers for sleeve until chart row 124 has been completed *and at the same time* inc 1 st at each end of 5th row and every foll 4th row until there are 80 sts, and then on every foll 5th row until there are 100 sts.
Bind off evenly.

to finish

Block pieces as explained on page 141.
Sew right shoulder seam, using backstitch.

Neckband

With RS facing and using size 3 (3.25mm) needles and yarn A, pick up and knit 24 sts down left front neck edge, 20 sts across center front neck edge, 24 sts up right front neck edge, and 40 sts across back neck edge. 108 sts.
Work 5 rows in garter st.
Bind off knitwise.
Sew left shoulder seam and neckband seam.
Sew sleeves to back and front, matching center of bound-off edge of sleeve to shoulder seam.
Sew side and sleeve seams.
Press seams lightly on WS, following instructions on yarn label and avoiding garter st.

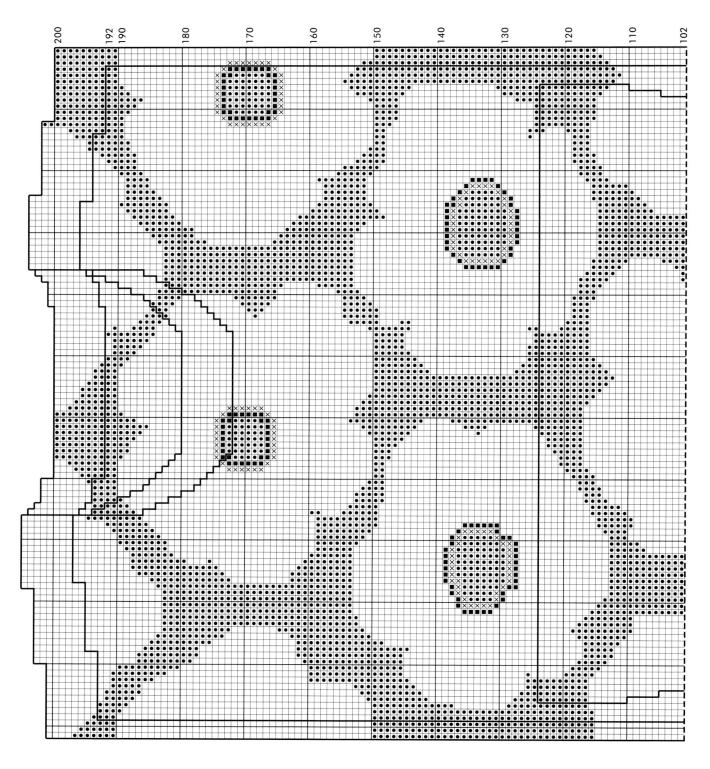

KEY

A ●
B □
C ✕
D ·
F ■

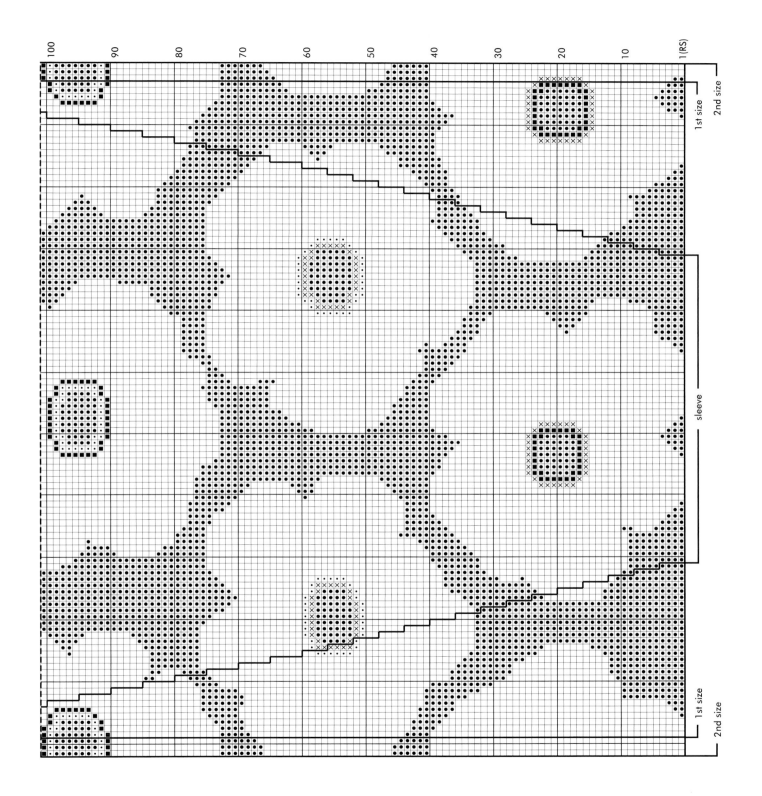

polka dots

sizes and measurements

To fit bust	32	34	36	38	40	in
	81	86	91	97	102	cm

Finished knitted measurements

Around bust	38	40	41	44	46	in
	96	101	105	112	116	cm
Length to shoulder	19	19½	19½	20	20½	in
	48	49	50	51	52	cm
Sleeve seam	17	17	17	17	17	in
	43	43	43	43	43	cm

yarn

Rowan *Cotton Glace* (50g/1¾oz per ball) as foll:

A	Ecru 725	5	5	6	6	7	balls
B	Sky 749	2	2	2	2	2	balls
C	Candy Floss 747	1	1	1	2	2	balls
D	Tickle 811	4	5	5	5	5	balls
E	Pier 809	2	2	3	3	3	balls
F	Hyacinth 787	3	3	4	4	4	balls

needles

Pair of size 2 (2.75mm) knitting needles
Pair of size 3 (3.25mm) knitting needles, *or size to obtain correct gauge*

gauge

26 sts and 32 rows to 4in/10cm measured over St st chart pattern using size 3 (3.25mm) needles. *Note: To save time, take time to check gauge.*

special chart note

When reading St st charts for back, fronts, and sleeves, read all odd-numbered RS (knit) rows from right to left and all even-numbered WS (purl) rows from left to right. When reading St st chart for front bands, read all odd-numbered WS (purl) rows from left to right and all even-numbered RS (knit) rows from right to left.

Use the intarsia technique for the vertical bands of background color, twisting yarns together on WS where they meet to avoid holes. Use the Fair Isle technique for the dots, weaving color not in use into back of work. To avoid weaving in lots of loose ends when knitting is complete, weave in ends on WS of knitting when joining in and cutting off yarns.

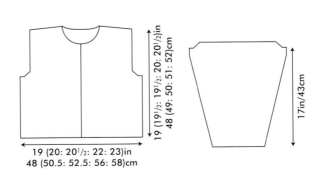

19 (19½: 19½: 20: 20½)in
48 (49: 50: 51: 52)cm

19 (20: 20½: 22: 23)in
48 (50.5: 52.5: 56: 58)cm

17in/43cm

back

Using size 2 (2.75mm) needles and yarn D, cast on 125 (131: 137: 145: 151) sts.

Work seed st border as foll:

Row 1 (RS) K1, *P1, K1, rep from * to end.

Rep last row 6 times, ending with a RS row.

Purl 1 row.

Change to size 3 (3.25mm) needles.

Set St st chart patt (see pages 66 and 67) on next 2 rows as foll:

Chart row 1 (RS) K to end, working 17 (20: 23: 27: 30)B, 30F, 31E, 30D, 17 (20: 23: 27: 30)C.

Chart row 2 P to end, working 17 (20: 23: 27: 30)C, 30D, 31E, 30F, 17 (20: 23: 27: 30)B.

Cont in St st chart patt as set until chart row 84 (84: 88: 88: 90) has been completed, ending with a WS row.

Shape armholes

Keeping chart patt correct throughout, bind off 4 sts at beg of next 2 rows. 117 (123: 129: 137: 143) sts.

Dec 1 st at each end of next 9 (9: 9: 11: 11) rows. 99 (105: 111: 115: 121) sts.

Work even until chart row 146 (148: 152: 156: 158) has been completed, ending with a WS row.

Shape shoulders and back neck

Bind off 10 (11: 12: 12: 13) sts at beg of next 2 rows. 79 (83: 87: 91: 95) sts.

Next row (RS) Bind off 10 (11: 12: 12: 13) sts, work in patt until there are 14 (15: 15: 17: 18) sts on right needle, then turn, leaving rem sts on a holder.

Cont on these 14 (15: 15: 17: 18) sts only for right side of neck.

Bind off 4 sts at beg of next row.

Bind off rem 10 (11: 11: 13: 14) sts.

With RS facing, rejoin yarn to rem sts on holder and bind off center 31 (31: 33: 33: 33) sts, then work in patt to end.

Complete to match first side, reversing shapings.

left front

Using size 2 (2.75mm) needles and yarn D, cast on 63 (65: 69: 73: 75) sts.

Work 7 rows in seed st as for back.

Purl 1 row, inc 0 (1: 0: 0: 1) st at center of row. 63 (66: 69: 73: 76) sts.

Change to size 3 (3.25mm) needles.

Beg with chart row 1, work in St st foll chart patt between markers for left front until chart row 84 (84: 88: 88: 90) has been completed, ending with a WS row.

Shape armhole

Keeping chart patt correct throughout, bind off 4 sts at beg of next row. 59 (62: 65: 69: 72) sts.

Work even for 1 row.

Dec 1 st at armhole edge of next 9 (9: 9: 11: 11) rows. 50 (53: 56: 58: 61) sts.

Work even until chart row 125 (127: 131: 135: 137) has been completed, ending with a RS row.

Shape neck

Bind off 10 (10: 11: 11: 11) sts at beg of next row, then 4 sts at beg of foll alt row. 36 (39: 41: 43: 46) sts.

Dec 1 st at neck edge on next 3 rows, then on foll 2 alt rows. 31 (34: 36: 38: 41) sts.

Work even for 3 rows.

Dec 1 st at neck edge on next row. 30 (33: 35: 37: 40) sts.

Work even for 7 rows, ending with chart row 146 (148: 152: 156: 158).

Shape shoulder

Bind off 10 (11: 12: 12: 13) sts at beg of next row and foll alt row.

Work even for 1 row.

Bind off rem 10 (11: 11: 13: 14) sts.

right front

Using size 2 (2.75mm) needles and yarn D, cast on 63 (65: 69: 73: 75) sts.

Work 7 rows in seed st as for back.

Purl 1 row, inc 0 (1: 0: 0: 1) st at center of row. 63 (66: 69: 73: 76) sts.

Change to size 3 (3.25mm) needles.

Beg with chart row 1, work in St st foll chart patt between markers for right front until chart row 85 (85: 89: 89: 91) has been completed, ending with a RS row.

Complete to match left front, reversing shapings.

sleeves (make 2)

Using size 2 (2.75mm) needles and yarn D, cast on 53 (53: 53: 57: 57) sts.

Work 7 rows in seed st as for back.

Purl 1 row.

Change to size 3 (3.25mm) needles.

Beg with chart row 1, work in St st foll chart patt for sleeve (see page 68) *and at the same time* inc 1 st at each end of 3rd row and every foll 4th row until there are 77 (89: 89: 93: 93) sts, then on every foll 6th row until there are 101 (105: 105: 109: 109) sts, taking inc sts into patt.

Keeping chart patt correct throughout, work even for 11 rows, thus ending with chart row 130.

Shape top of sleeve

Bind off 4 sts at beg of next 2 rows. 93 (97: 97: 101: 101) sts.

Dec 1 st at each end of next row and foll 8 alt rows.

Work even for 1 row, ending with a WS row.

Bind off rem 75 (79: 79: 83: 83) sts.

to finish

Block pieces as explained on page 141.
Sew shoulder seams, using backstitch.

Right front band

With RS facing and using size 3 (3.25mm)
needles, pick up and knit 107 (107: 113:
119: 119) sts up right front center edge
using yarns as foll:
18 (18: 24: 24: 24)B, 23F, 25E, 24D, 17
(17: 17: 23: 23)C.
Beg with chart row 1 (a P row), work 7 rows
in patt from chart for right front band (see
opposite page), ending with a WS row.
Change to size 2 (2.75mm) needles and
yarn D.
Knit 2 rows (the second of these 2 rows
forms fold line).
Beg with a K row, work 2 rows in St st.
Cut off yarn D.
Using yarn B, work 5 rows more in St st.
Bind off.
Fold band to WS along fold line and slip
stitch in place.

Left front band

With RS facing and using size 3 (3.25mm)
needles, pick up and knit 107 (107: 113:
119: 119) sts down left front center edge
using yarns as foll:
17 (17: 17: 23: 23)C, 24D, 25E, 23F, 18
(18: 24: 24: 24)B.
Turn right front band chart upside down and,
beg with chart row 1 (a P row), work 7 rows
in patt from chart for left front band, ending
with a WS row. (The positions for the color
blocks are reversed to mirror those of the
right front band.)
Complete to match right front band.

Collar

Using size 2 (2.75mm) needles and yarn D,
cast on 115 (115: 119: 119: 119) sts.
Work 3in/7.5cm in seed st as for back.
Bind off loosely and evenly in seed st.
Positioning row ends of collar midway across
top of front bands, sew cast-on edge of
collar to neck edge.
Sew side seams. Sew sleeve seams, then set
in sleeves, matching center of top of sleeve to
shoulder seam.
Press seams lightly on WS, following
instructions on yarn label.

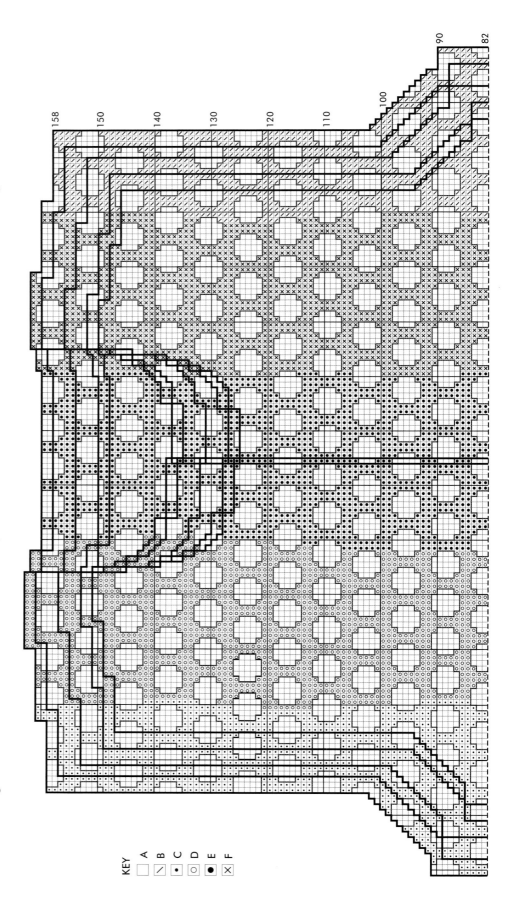

KEY A □ B / C • D ○ E ● F ✕

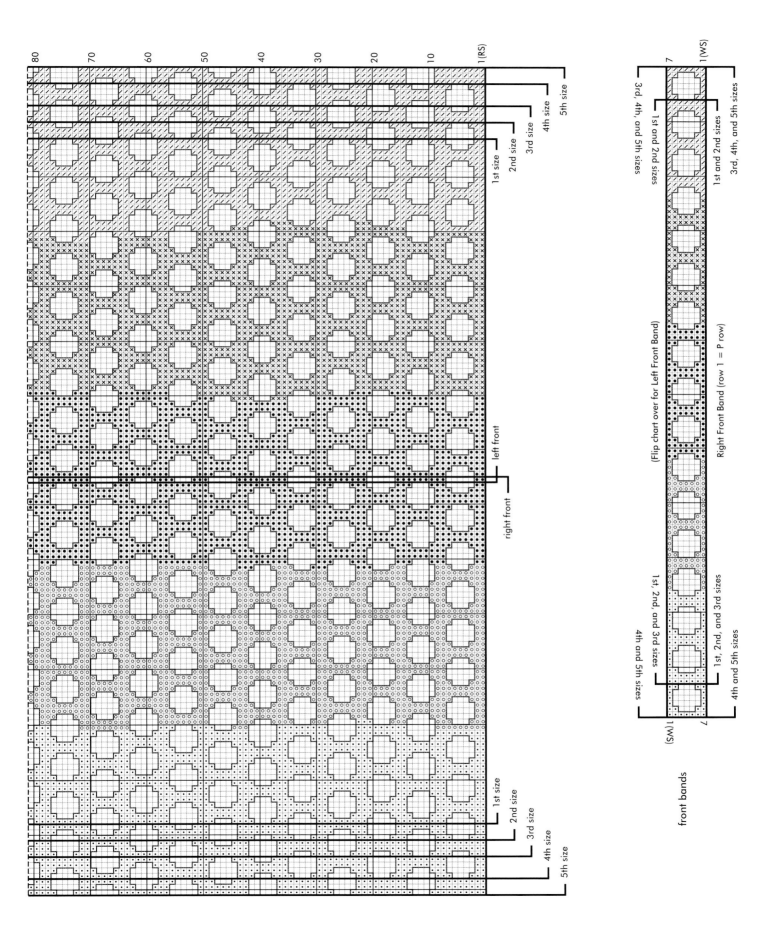

front bands

polka dots 67

☐ A
╲ B
· C
◯ D
● E
☒ F

150
140
130
120
110
100
90
80
70
60
50
40
30
20
10
1 (RS)

1st, 2nd, and 3rd sizes sleeve
4th and 5th sizes sleeve

chinese lanterns

size and measurements

To fit bust   36–40in/91–102cm

Finished knitted measurements

Around bust	44in/112cm
Length to shoulder	21in/53.5cm
Sleeve seam	19in/49cm

yarn

Rowan *Cotton Glace* (50g/1¾oz per ball) as foll:

A	Sky 749	9 balls
B	Hot Lips 818	1 ball
C	Candy Floss 747	2 balls
D	Tickle 811	2 balls
E	Oyster 730	1 ball
F	Bleached 726	1 ball
G	Hyacinth 787	2 balls

needles

Pair of size 2 (2.75mm) knitting needles
Pair of size 3 (3.25mm) knitting needles, *or size to obtain correct gauge*
Size 2 (2.75mm) circular knitting needle, 32in/80cm long

extras

5 buttons

gauge

23 sts and 32 rows to 4in/10cm measured over St st chart pattern using size 3 (3.25mm) needles. *Note: To save time, take time to check gauge.*

special chart note

When reading St st chart, read all odd-numbered RS (knit) rows from right to left and all even-numbered WS (purl) rows from left to right. Use the intarsia technique, using a separate length of yarn for each area of color and twisting yarns together on WS where they meet to avoid holes.

To avoid weaving in lots of loose ends when knitting is complete, weave in ends on WS of knitting when joining in and cutting off yarns.

Note that the chart includes the color pattern for the widest part of the cardigan; but when beginning the back and front pieces, work within the side-edge outlines.

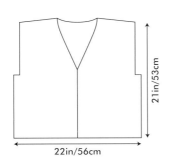

21in/53cm

22in/56cm

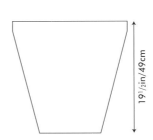

19½in/49cm

back

Using size 2 (2.75mm) needles and yarn G, cast on 117 sts.
Join in yarn A and work 2-color rib as foll:
Rib row 1 (RS) K3G, *P3A, K3G, rep from * to end.
Rib row 2 P3G, *K3A, P3G, rep from * to end.
Rep rib rows 1 and 2 twice more, ending with a WS row.
Cut off yarn G.
Change to size 3 (3.25mm) needles.
Using yarn A and beg with a K row, work 10 rows in St st (these are first 10 rows on chart), ending with a WS row.
Set St st chart patt on next 2 rows as foll:
Chart row 11 (RS) K to end, working 7A, 3B, *17A, 3B, rep from * to last 7 sts, 7A.
Chart row 12 P to end, working 5A, 7B, *13A, 7B, rep from * to last 5 sts, 5A.
Cont in St st chart patt as set, repeating 42-row patt rep throughout, *and at the same time* shape side edges by inc 1 st at each end on chart row 17 and every foll 10th row until there are 129 sts.
Keeping patt correct throughout, work even until *2 patt reps* have been completed, ending with a chart row 46 (a WS row)—88 St st patt rows have been completed after ribbing.

Shape armhole
Bind off 8 sts at beg of next 2 rows. 113 sts.
Cont in patt until armhole measures 9½in/24cm from armhole bind-off, ending with a WS row.

Shape shoulders and back neck
Bind off 12 sts at beg of next 2 rows.
Next row (RS) Bind off 13 sts, work in patt until there are 17 sts on right needle, then turn, leaving rem sts on a holder.
Cont on these 17 sts only for right side of neck.
Bind off 4 sts at beg of next row.
Bind off rem 13 sts.
With RS facing, rejoin yarn to rem sts and bind off center 29 sts, then work in patt to end.
Complete to match first side, reversing shapings.

left front

Using size 2 (2.75mm) needles and yarn G, cast on 59 sts.
Join in yarn A and work 2-color rib as foll:
Rib row 1 (RS) *K3G, P3A, rep from * to last 5 sts, K3G, P2A.
Rib row 2 K2A, P3G, *K3A, P3G, rep from * to end.
Rep rib rows 1 and 2 twice more, ending with a WS row.

Cut off yarn G.
Change to size 3 (3.25mm) needles.
Using yarn A and beg with a K row, work 10 rows in St st (these are first 10 rows on chart), ending with a WS row.
Beg with chart row 11, cont in patt foll chart between markers for left front, repeating 42-row patt rep throughout, *and at the same time* shape side edge by inc 1 st at side edge on chart row 17 and every foll 10th row until there are 65 sts.
Keeping patt correct throughout, work even until left front matches back to armhole shaping, ending with a WS row.

Shape armhole
Bind off 8 sts at beg of next row. 57 sts.
Work even in patt for 7 rows.

Shape front neck
Dec 1 st at neck edge on next row and every foll 3rd row until 38 sts rem.
Work even until front matches back to beg of shoulder shaping, ending with a WS row.

Shape shoulder
Bind off 12 sts at beg of next row. 26 sts.
Work even for 1 row.
Bind off 13 sts at beg of next row.
Work even for 1 row.
Bind off rem 13 sts.

right front

Using size 2 (2.75mm) needles and yarn G, cast on 59 sts.
Join in yarn A and work 2-color rib as foll:
Rib row 1 (RS) P2A, K3G, *P3A, K3G, rep from * to end.
Rib row 2 *P3G, K3A, rep from * to last 5 sts, P3G, K2A.
Rep rib rows 1 and 2 twice more, ending with a WS row.
Complete as for left front, following chart between markers for right front and reversing shapings.

sleeves (make 2)

Using size 2 (2.75mm) needles and yarn G, cast on 57 sts.
Join in yarn A and work 6 rows in 2-color rib as for back.
Cut off yarn G.
Change to size 3 (3.25mm) needles.
Using yarn A and beg with a K row, work 10 rows in St st (these are first 10 rows on chart), ending with a WS row, *and at the same time* inc 1 st at each end of 7th row.

Beg with chart row 11, cont in patt foll chart between markers for sleeve, repeating 42-row patt rep throughout, *and at the same time* shape side edges by inc 1 st at each end on chart row 11 and every foll 4th row until there are 77 sts, and then on every foll 6th row until there are 109 sts.

Keeping patt correct throughout, work even until sleeve measures 19in/49cm from cast-on edge, ending with a WS row.

Bind off loosely and evenly.

to finish

Block pieces as explained on page 141.

Sew both shoulder seams, using backstitch.

Front band

With RS of right front facing and using size 2 (2.75mm) circular needle and yarn A, pick up and knit 75 sts up front from cast-on edge to beg of front neck shaping, 58 sts up to shoulder, 36 sts across back neck, 58 sts down left front to beg of front neck shaping, and 75 sts to cast-on edge. 302 sts.

Row 1 (WS) P to end.

Row 2 (buttonhole row) (RS) K4, [bind off 3 sts, K until there are 14 sts on right needle after last bind-off] 4 times, bind off 3 sts,

K to end.

Row 3 P to end, casting on 3 sts over those bound off on previous row.

Row 4 K to end.

Cut off yarn A and change to yarn G.

Row 5 P to end.

Row 6 P to end, to form fold line.

Row 7 P to end.

Row 8 Rep row 2

Row 9 Rep row 3.

Cont in St st for 4 rows more.

Bind off loosely and evenly.

Fold band to WS along fold line and slip stitch in place.

Sew sleeves to armholes, matching center of bound-off edge of sleeve to shoulder seam and sewing bound-off edge of sleeve top to straight vertical edge of armhole and last 1¼in/3.5cm of side edge of sleeve to 8 bound-off sts at underarm.

Sew side and sleeve seams.

Press seams lightly on WS, following instructions on yarn label and avoiding ribbing.

KEY

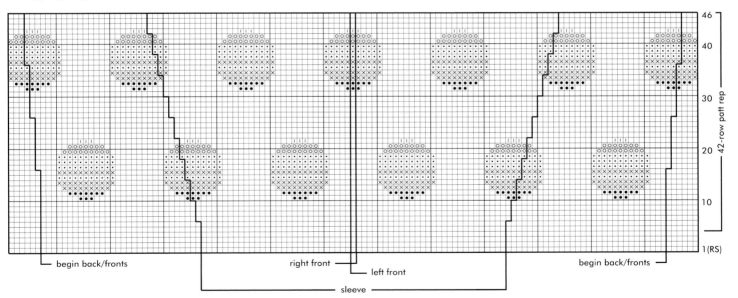

begin back/fronts   right front —   left front   begin back/fronts

sleeve

moody blues cushion

size

Finished cushion measures approximately 19in/47.5cm wide by 18¾in/47cm tall.

yarn

Rowan *Scottish Tweed 4-Ply* (25g/⅞oz per ball) as foll:

A	Lavender 005	1 ball
B	Peat 019	1 ball
C	Sea Green 006	1 ball
D	Lobster 017	1 ball
E	Thatch 018	1 ball
F	Midnight 023	1 ball
G	Rust 009	1 ball
H	Thistle 016	1 ball
J	Lewis Grey 007	1 ball
L	Wine 012	1 ball
M	Herring 008	1 ball
N	Claret 013	1 ball
Q	Mallard 020	1 ball
R	Apple 015	1 ball
S	Sunset 011	1 ball
T	Brilliant Pink 010	1 ball
U	Winter Navy 021	1 ball
V	Skye 003	1 ball

needles

Pair of size 5 (3.75mm) knitting needles, *or size to obtain correct gauge*

extras

Pillow form to fit finished cover
Fabric and matching thread, for backing

gauge

21 sts and 32 rows to 4in/10cm measured over St st chart pattern using size 5 (3.75mm) needles. *Note: To save time, take time to check gauge.*

special chart note

When reading St st chart, read all odd-numbered RS (knit rows) from right to left and all even-numbered WS (purl rows) from left to right.
Use the intarsia technique, using a separate length of yarn for each area of color and twisting yarns together on WS where they meet to avoid holes.
To avoid weaving in lots of loose ends when knitting is complete, weave in ends on WS of knitting when joining in and cutting off yarns.

to make cushion front

Using size 5 (3.75mm) needles and yarn J, cast on 100 sts.
Set St st chart patt on next 2 rows as foll:
Chart row 1 (RS) K to end, working 1A, 5B, 19C, 19D, 5E, 1F, 1G, 5H, 19J, 19D, 5A, 1B.
Chart row 2 (WS) P to end, working 1B, 5A, 19D, 19J, 5H, 1G, 1F, 5E, 19D, 19C, 5B, 1A.
Cont in St st chart patt as set until all 150 rows of chart have been completed, ending with a WS (P) row.
Using yarn J, bind off.

to finish

Block knitting as explained on page 141.
Cut piece of fabric to same size as knitted front, plus ½in/1.5cm extra all around for seam allowances. With RS together, sew backing to knitted front, leaving one side open.
Turn right side out and insert pillow form. Sew opening closed.
Alternatively, make backing in two separate pieces to make an "envelope" backing (with the two pieces overlapping by 5–6in/13–15cm at center) so that the pillow form can be removed easily.

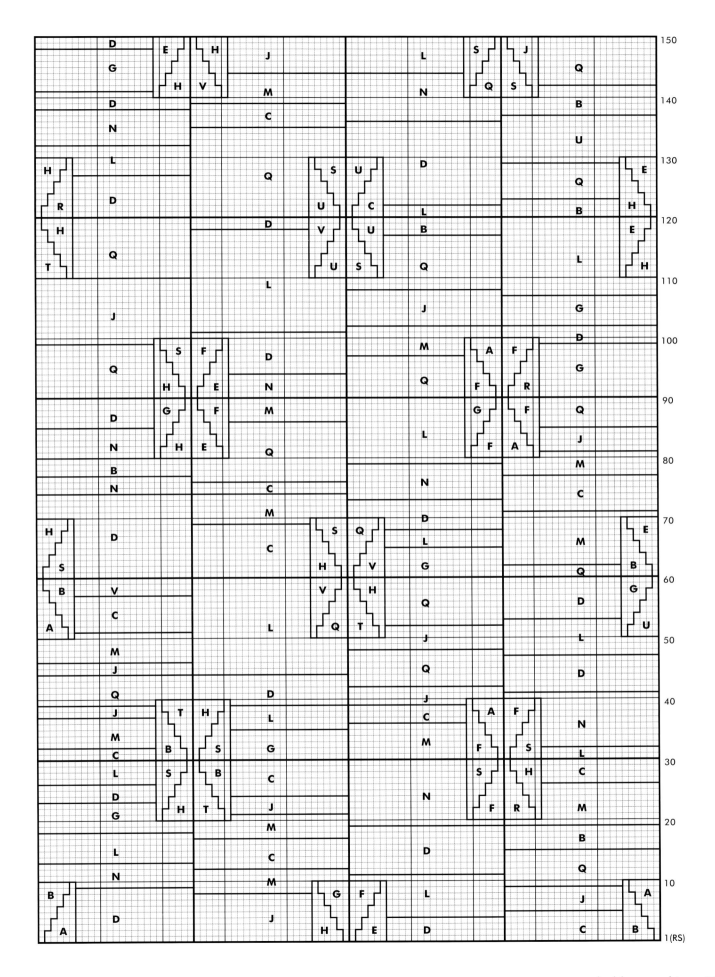

cheviot gardens

size and measurements

To fit bust   34–38in/86–97cm

Finished knitted measurements

Around bust	40in/101cm
Length to shoulder	21½in/54.5cm
Sleeve seam	19½in/49cm

yarn

Rowan *Handknit Cotton* (50g/1¾oz per ball) as foll:

A	Diana 287	2 balls
B	Flame 254	1 ball
C	Sugar 303	1 ball
D	Gooseberry 219	9 balls
E	Decadent 314	2 balls
F	Slippery 316	5 balls
G	Seafarer 318	1 ball
H	Lupin 305	1 ball
J	Shell 310	1 ball

needles

Pair of size 3 (3.25mm) knitting needles
Pair of size 6 (4mm) knitting needles, *or size to obtain correct gauge*
Size 3 (3.25mm) circular knitting needle, 32in/80cm long

extras

5 buttons

gauge

22 sts and 25 rows to 4in/10cm measured over St st chart pattern using size 6 (4mm) needles. *Note: To save time, take time to check gauge.*

special chart note

When reading St st chart, read all odd-numbered RS (knit) rows from right to left and all even-numbered WS (purl) rows from left to right. Use the Fair Isle technique, weaving color not in use into back of work.

To avoid weaving in lots of loose ends when knitting is complete, weave in ends on WS of knitting when joining in and cutting off yarns.

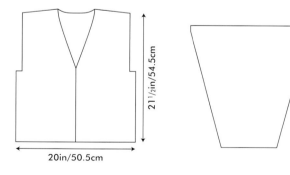

back

Using size 3 (3.25mm) needles and yarn F, cast on 111 sts.
Beg with a K row, work 10 rows in St st, ending with a WS row.
Next row (RS) P to end, to form fold line.
Next row (inc row) P11, [M1, P10] 10 times. 121 sts.
Change to size 6 (4mm) needles.
Beg St st color patt from chart row 1 (see pages 76 and 77) and

working between markers for back, work until chart row 64 has been completed, ending with a WS row.

Shape armholes

Keeping chart patt correct throughout, bind off 9 sts at beg of next 2 rows. 103 sts.

Work even until chart row 126 has been completed, ending with a WS row.

Shape shoulders and back neck

Bind off 11 sts at beg of next 2 rows.

Next row (RS) Bind off 12 sts, work in patt until there are 16 sts on right needle, then turn, leaving rem sts on a holder.

Cont on these 16 sts only for right side of neck.

Bind off 4 sts at beg of next row.

Bind off rem 12 sts.

With RS facing, rejoin yarn to rem sts and bind off center 25 sts, then work in patt to end.

Complete to match first side, reversing shapings.

pocket linings (make 2)

Using size 6 (4mm) needles and yarn D, cast on 22 sts.
Beg with a K row, work 21 rows in St st, ending with a RS row.
Next row (inc row) (WS) P across row, inc 3 sts evenly across row. 25 sts.
Leave sts on a holder.

left front

Using size 3 (3.25mm) needles and yarn F, cast on 56 sts.
Beg with a K row, work 10 rows in St st, ending with a WS row.
Next row (RS) P to end, to form fold line.
Next row (inc row) P6, [M1, P10] 5 times. 61 sts.
Change to size 6 (4mm) needles.
Beg St st color patt from chart row 1 and working between markers for left front, work until chart row 30 has been completed, ending with a WS row.

Place pocket lining

Chart row 31 (RS) Work first 15 sts in patt, slip next 25 sts onto a holder and work in patt across 25 sts of first pocket lining, work last 21 sts in patt.
Cont in chart patt until chart row 64 has been completed, ending with a WS row.

Shape armhole

Keeping chart patt correct throughout, bind off 9 sts at beg of next row. 52 sts.
Work even for 3 rows.

Shape front neck

Dec 1 st at neck edge on next row and every foll 3rd row until 35 sts rem.
Work even until front matches back to shoulder shaping, ending with a WS row.

Shape shoulder

Bind off 11 sts at beg of next row and 12 sts at beg of foll alt row.
Work 1 row even.
Bind off rem 12 sts.

right front

Work as for left front, but following chart between markers for right front and reversing shapings and pocket placement.

sleeves (make 2)

Using size 3 (3.25mm) needles and yarn F, cast on 45 sts.
Beg with a K row, work 10 rows in St st, ending with a WS row.
Next row (RS) P to end, to form fold line.
Next row (inc row) P9, [M1, P9] 4 times. 49 sts.
Change to size 6 (4mm) needles.
Beg St st color patt from chart row 1 and working between markers for sleeve, work until chart row 120 has been completed *and at the same time* inc 1 st at each end of 11th row and every foll alt row until there are 77 sts, and then on every foll 4th row until there are 111 sts.
Bind off.

to finish

Block pieces as explained on page 141.
Sew both shoulder seams, using backstitch.

Button band

With RS of right front facing and using size 3 (3.25mm) circular needle and yarn D, pick up and knit 54 sts up front from hemline fold to beg of front neck shaping, 50 sts up to shoulder, 31 sts across back neck, 50 sts down left front to beg of front neck shaping, and 54 sts to hemline fold. 239 sts.
Row 1 (WS) Using yarns D and E, *P3D, P1E, rep from * to last 3 sts, P3D.
Cut off yarn E.
Row 2 (buttonhole row) (RS) Using yarn D, K2, [K2tog, yo twice, K2tog, K8] 4 times, K2tog, yo twice, K2tog, K to end.
Cut off yarn D.
Row 3 Using yarn F, P across row, working into back loops of yarn overs made for buttonholes in previous row.
Row 4 Using yarns F and C, *K1C, K3F, rep from * to last 2 sts, K1C, K1F.
Cut off yarn C.
Row 5 Using yarn F, P to end.
Cut off yarn F.
Using yarn A, complete as foll:
K 1 row.
Next row (WS) K to end, to form fold line.
Beg with a K row, work 8 rows in St st, working buttonholes on 3rd of these rows (a RS row) to correspond with those made previously.
Bind off loosely.

Pocket tops

With RS facing and using size 3 (3.25mm) needles and yarn F, K across 25 sts on holder for first pocket top.
Next row (WS) K to end, to form fold line.
Beg with a K row, work 4 rows in St st.
Bind off.
Work second pocket top in same way.
Sew sleeves to armholes, matching center of bound-off edge of sleeve to shoulder seam and sewing bound-off edge of sleeve top to straight vertical edge of armhole and last 1¾in/4cm of side edge of sleeve to 9 bound-off sts at underarm.
Sew side and sleeve seams.
Fold button band and all hems to WS along fold line and slip stitch in place.
Press seams lightly on WS, following instructions on yarn label.
Sew on buttons to correspond with buttonholes.

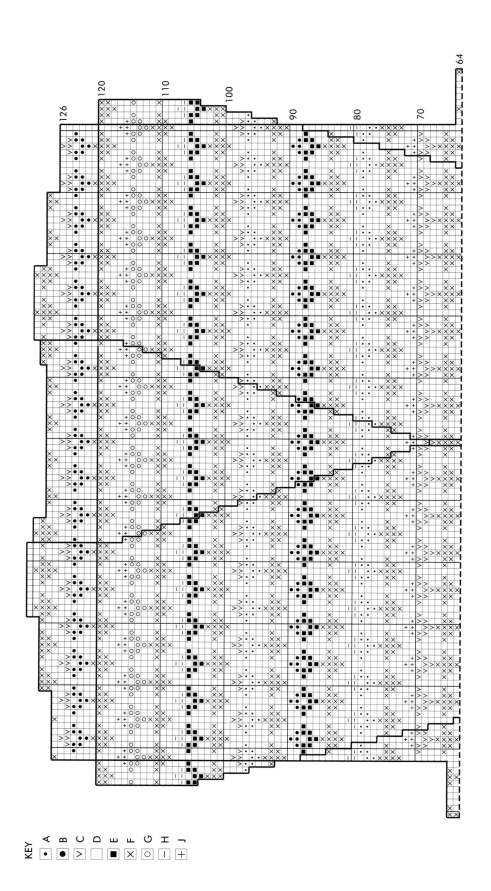

KEY

A	B	C	D	E	F	G	H	J
•	●	>	☐	■	✕	○	I	+

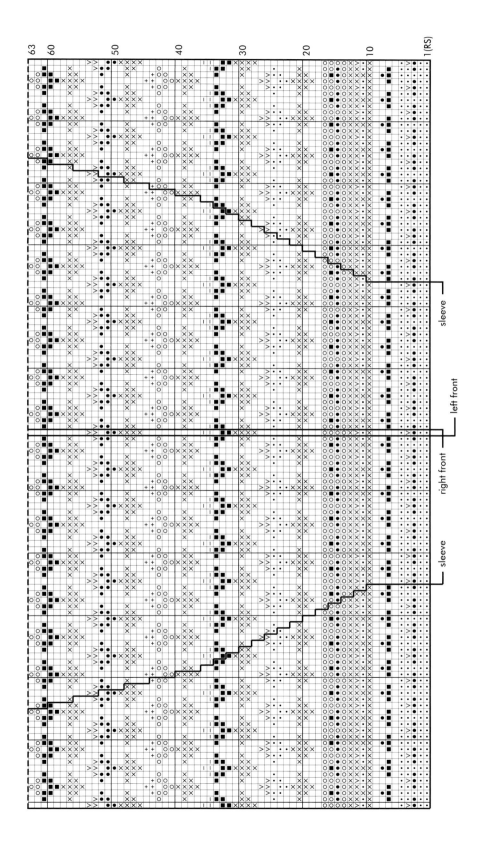

domino cushion

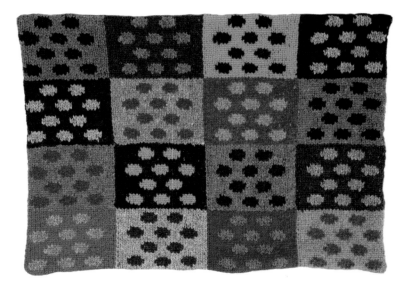

size
Finished cushion measures approximately 24in/61cm wide by 18in/45.5cm tall.

yarn
Rowan *Scottish Tweed 4-Ply* (25g/⅞oz per ball) as foll:

A	Sunset 011	1 ball
B	Claret 013	1 ball
C	Skye 003	1 ball
D	Wine 012	1 ball
E	Lobster 017	1 ball
F	Sea Green 006	1 ball
G	Mallard 020	1 ball
H	Lavender 005	1 ball
J	Apple 015	1 ball
L	Winter Navy 021	1 ball
M	Thatch 018	1 ball
N	Thistle 016	1 ball
Q	Brilliant Pink 010	1 ball

needles
Pair of size 8 (5mm) knitting needles, *or size to obtain correct gauge*

extras
Pillow form to fit finished cover
Fabric and matching thread, for backing

gauge
18 sts and 23 rows to 4in/10cm measured over St st chart pattern using size 8 (5mm) needles and two strands of yarn. *Note: To save time, take time to check gauge.*

special yarn note
Use two strands of yarn held together throughout.

special chart note
When reading St st chart, read all odd-numbered RS (knit) rows from right to left and all even-numbered WS (purl) rows from left to right. Use the intarsia technique for individual squares, using a separate length of yarn for each area of color and twisting yarns together on WS where they meet to avoid holes. Within each square use the Fair Isle technique, weaving color not in use into back of work. To avoid weaving in lots of loose ends when knitting is complete, weave in ends on WS of knitting when joining in and cutting off yarns.

to make cushion front

Using size 8 (5mm) needles and two strands of each yarn held tog, cast on 27 sts each in yarns D, C, B, and A (in this order) for a total of 108 sts.

Set St st chart patt on next 3 rows as foll:

Chart row 1 (RS) K to end, working 27A, 27B, 27C, 27D.
Chart row 2 (WS) P to end, working 27D, 27C, 27B, 27A.
Chart row 3 (WS) K to end, working 4A, [3E, 5A] twice, 3E, 4A, 4B, [3F, 5B] twice, 3F, 4B, 4C, [3G, 5C] twice, 3G, 4C, 4D, [3H, 5D] twice, 3H, 4D.

Cont in St st in chart patt as set, foll motif chart for patt in each 27-st square and color diagram for background and dot-motif colors, until chart row 26 has been completed, ending with a WS row.

Cut off all yarns.

Joining in and cutting off yarns as required, work rem 3 rows of 4 squares in same way, foll motif chart for patt in each square and color diagram for colors, until all 104 rows have been completed, ending with a WS (P) row.
Bind off.

to finish

Block knitting as explained on page 141.

Cut piece of fabric to same size as knitted front, plus ½in/1.5cm extra all around for seam allowances. With RS together, sew backing to knitted front, leaving one side open.

Turn right side out and insert pillow form. Sew opening closed. Alternatively, make backing in two separate pieces to make an "envelope" backing (with the two pieces overlapping by 5–6in/ 13–15cm at center) so that the pillow form can be removed easily.

note: Follow this diagram for the colors on the Domino Cushion. Each square on the diagram represents one of the 16 squares of the design and one chart repeat. The background color is given in each square, with the dot color in a circle.

dot motif and background colors

L / F	J / G	L / Q	C / N
C / N	B / H	A / E	L / M
B / M	Q / L	N / J	H / G
H / D	G / C	F / B	E / A

dot motif chart

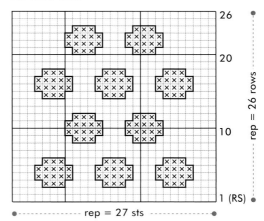

26

20

10

1 (RS)

rep = 26 rows

rep = 27 sts

brocade throw

size
Finished throw measures approximately 41½in/104cm wide by 46in/115cm long, including garter st border.

yarns
Rowan *Handknit Cotton* (50g/1¾oz per ball) as foll:

A	Tope 253	3 balls
B	Ice Water 239	4 balls
C	Diana 287	3 balls
D	Gooseberry 219	3 balls
E	Slippery 316	2 balls
F	Slick 313	3 balls
G	Lupin 305	3 balls
H	Rosso 215	2 balls
J	Fruit Salad 203	1 ball
L	Flame 254	1 ball
M	Seafarer 318	1 ball
N	Celery 309	1 ball
Q	Mojito 322	1 ball

needles
Size 7 (4.5mm) long circular knitting needle, *or size to obtain correct gauge*
Size 6 (4mm) long circular needle for border

gauge
20 sts and 23½ rows to 4in/10cm measured over St st chart pattern using size 7 (4.5mm) needles. *Note: To save time, take time to check gauge.*

special chart note
When reading St st charts, read all odd-numbered RS (knit) rows from right to left and all even-numbered WS (purl) rows from left to right. Use the Fair Isle technique, weaving color not in use into back of work.

To avoid weaving in lots of loose ends when knitting is complete, weave in ends on WS of knitting when joining in and cutting off yarns.

to make throw
Using size 6 (4mm) circular needle and yarn B, cast on 206 sts. Working back and forth in rows on circular needle, work border in garter st (K every row) as foll:
Row 1 (RS) K to end.
Row 2 (dec row) K2tog, K to last 2 sts, K2tog. 204 sts.
Rep last 2 rows once more. 202 sts.
Cut off yarn B.
Using yarn C, rep last 2 rows once more. 200 sts.

Cut off yarn C.
Change to size 7 (4.5mm) circular needle and working back and forth in rows on circular needle, work color patt in St st as foll:
Stripe 1
Using yarn A for background color and yarn B for motif color and beg with a K row, work rows 1–15 of chart 1 (see pages 82 and 83), ending with a RS row.
Cut off yarns A and B.

Stripe 2

Slide sts back to other end of needle to beg next row with RS facing.

Using yarn C for background color and yarn D for motif color, work rows 1–20 of chart 2, ending with a WS row.

Cut off yarns C and D.

Stripe 3

Using yarn E for background color and yarn F for motif color, work rows 7–22 of chart 3, ending with a WS row.

Cut off yarns E and F.

Stripe 4

Using yarn B for background color and yarn G for motif color, work rows 1–20 of chart 3, ending with a WS row.

Cut off yarns B and G.

Stripe 5

Using yarn H for background color and yarn A for motif color, work rows 1–15 of chart 2, ending with a RS row.

Cut off yarns H and A.

Stripe 6

Slide sts back to other end of needle to beg next row with RS facing.

Using yarn E for background color and yarn J for motif color, work rows 1–15 of chart 1.

Cut off yarn E.

Using yarn Q for background color and yarn J for motif color, work rows 16–21 of chart 1, ending with a RS row.

Cut off yarns Q and J.

Stripe 7

Slide sts back to other end of needle to beg next row with RS facing.

Using yarn F for background color and yarn D for motif color, work rows 1–14 of chart 2, ending with a WS row.

Cut off yarns F and D.

Stripe 8

Using yarn C for background color and yarn G for motif color, work rows 1–20 of chart 3, ending with a WS row.

Cut off yarns C and G.

Stripe 9

Using yarn H for background color and yarn D for the motif color, work rows 1–12 of chart 1.

Cut off yarn H.

Using yarn L for background color and yarn D for the motif color, work rows 13–15 of chart 1, ending with a RS row.

Cut off yarns L and D.

Stripe 10

Slide sts back to other end of needle to beg next row with RS facing.

Using yarn A for background color and yarn M for motif color, work rows 1–20 of chart 2, ending with a WS row.

Cut off yarns A and M.

Stripe 11

Using yarn E for background color and yarn G for motif color, work rows 1–15 of chart 3, ending with a RS row.

Cut off yarns E and G.

Stripe 12

Slide sts back to other end of needle to beg next row with RS facing.

Using yarn F for background color and yarn N for motif color, work rows 1–20 of chart 1, ending with a WS row.

Cut off yarns F and N.

Stripe 13

Using yarn B for background color and yarn L for motif color, work rows 1–15 of chart 2, ending with a RS row.

Cut off yarns B and L.

Stripe 14

Slide sts back to other end of needle to beg next row with RS facing.

Using yarn A for background color and yarn D for motif color, work rows 1–20 of chart 3, ending with a WS row.

Cut off yarns A and D.

Stripe 15

Using yarn B for background color and yarn G for motif color, work rows 1–16 of chart 1, ending with a WS row.

Cut off yarns B and G.

Top border

Change to size 6 (4mm) circular needle and work garter st border as foll:

Next row (RS) Using yarn C, K to end.

**Next row (inc row) (WS) Using yarn C, K into front and back of first st, K to last 2 sts, K into front and back of next st, K1.

Cut off yarn C.

Using yarn B, rep last 2 rows twice. 206 sts.

Bind off loosely knitwise.**

to finish

Block knitting as explained on page 141.

Side borders

Working back and forth in rows on circular needle, work garter st border along each side edge as foll:

With RS facing and using size 6 (4mm) circular needle and yarn C, pick up and knit 220 sts along side edge (picking up 11 sts for every 13 rows).

Complete border as for top border from ** to **.

Sew together mitered ends of borders at corners.

note: Each of the three charts is split down the center and positioned across two pages, so be sure to work each row across the entire chart.

chart 1

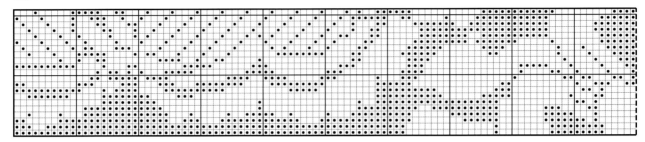

chart 2

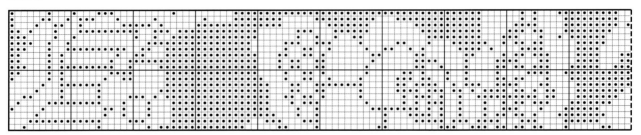

chart 3

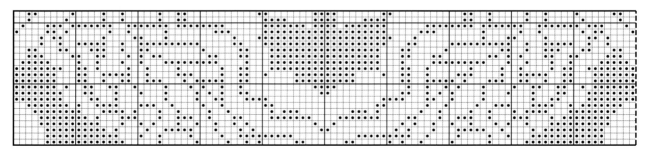

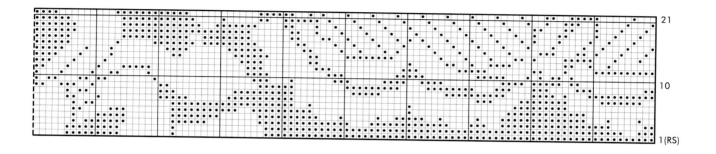

21

10

1 (RS)

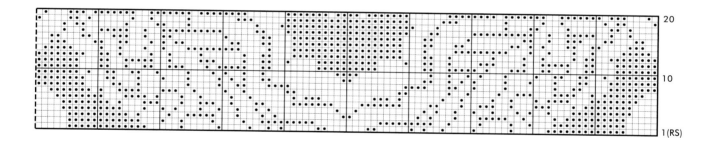

20

10

1 (RS)

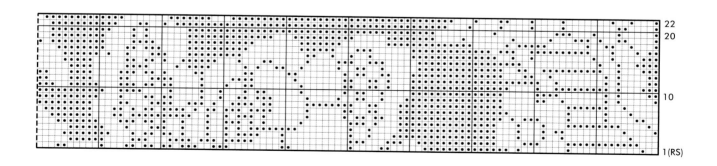

22
20

10

1 (RS)

squiggle stripe

sizes and measurements

To fit bust	32–34	36	38	in
	81–86	91	97	cm

Finished knitted measurements

Around bust	36	38	40	in
	90	95	100	cm
Length to shoulder	19¼	19¼	19¼	in
	48	48	48	cm

yarn

Rowan *Cotton Glace* (50g/1¾oz per ball) as foll:

A	Candy Floss 747	3	3	3	balls
B	Sky 749	2	2	3	balls
C	Hyacinth 787	2	3	3	balls
D	Tickle 811	1	1	1	ball
E	Oyster 730	1	1	1	ball
F	Butter 795	1	1	1	ball
G	Ecru 725	1	1	1	ball

Rowan *4-Ply Cotton* (50g/1¾oz per ball) as foll:

H	Ardour 130	1	1	1	ball
J	Orchid 120	1	1	1	ball
L	Ripple 121	1	1	1	ball
M	Fresh 131	1	1	1	ball

needles

Pair of size 2 (2.75mm) knitting needles
Pair of size 3 (3.25mm) knitting needles, *or size to obtain correct gauge*
Size 2 (2.75mm) circular knitting needle, 32in/80cm long

extras

6 buttons

gauge

32 sts and 34 rows to 4in/10cm measured over St st chart pattern using size 3 (3.25mm) needles. *Note: To save time, take time to check gauge.*

special chart note

When reading St st chart, read all odd-numbered RS (knit) rows from right to left and all even-numbered WS (purl) rows from left to right. Use the Fair Isle technique, weaving colors not in use into back of work. Only two colors are used in each row—the squiggle color (yarn C) and the background stripe color (see stripe sequence table). To avoid weaving in lots of loose ends when knitting is complete, weave in ends on WS of knitting when joining in and cutting off yarns.

19¼in/48cm

18 (19: 20)in/45 (47.5: 50)cm

back

Using size 2 (2.75mm) needles and yarn A, cast on 112 (120: 128) sts.
Beg with a K row, work 10 rows in St st, ending with a WS row.
Next row (RS) P to end, to form fold line.
Next row P to end.
Change to size 3 (3.25mm) needles.
Set St st chart patt (see pages 86 and 87) on next 2 rows as foll:
Chart row 1 (RS) K across row, working 0 (0: 2)B, 0 (0: 2)C, 0 (1: 1)B, 0 (1: 1)C, 1 (3: 3)B, [2C, 2B, 1C, 3B, 1C, 2B, 3C, 3B, 2C, 1B, 1C, 3B] 4 times, 2C, 2B, 1C, 3B, 1C, 2B, 3C, 1 (3: 3)B, 0 (2: 2)C, 0 (0: 1)B, 0 (0: 1)C, 0 (0: 2)B.

stripe sequence table

Starting with chart row 1, work background stripe patt in St st beg with a K row in stripe sequence as foll:

Chart rows 1–4 4 rows B.
Chart rows 5–6 2 rows H.
Chart row 7 1 row A.
Chart rows 8–9 2 rows D.
Chart rows 10–12 3 rows J.
Chart row 13 1 row E.
Chart rows 14–15 2 rows L.
Chart row 16 1 row B.
Chart rows 17–18 2 rows A.
Chart rows 19–21 3 rows F.
Chart row 22 1 row L.
Chart rows 23–24 2 rows M.
Chart rows 25–26 2 rows G.
Chart rows 27–29 3 rows L.
Chart rows 30–31 2 rows B.
Chart row 32 1 row A.

Chart row 33 1 row H.
Chart row 34 1 row F.
Chart rows 35–37 3 rows A.
Chart rows 38–39 2 rows D.
Chart row 40 1 row J.
Chart rows 41–42 2 rows E.
Chart row 43 1 row G.
Chart rows 44–45 2 rows M.
Chart row 46 1 row A.
Chart row 47 1 row B.
Chart row 48 1 row D.
Chart rows 49–50 2 rows J.
Chart rows 51–53 3 rows L.
Chart rows 54–55 2 rows F.
Chart row 56 1 row J.
Chart row 57 1 row H.

Chart rows 58–59 2 rows B.
Chart rows 60–61 2 rows A.
Chart row 62 1 row L.
Chart row 63 1 row E.
Chart rows 64–66 3 rows M.
Chart row 67 1 row A.
Chart row 68 1 row D.
Chart rows 69–70 2 rows J.
Chart rows 71–72 2 rows G.
Chart row 73 1 row E.
Chart rows 74–75 2 rows L.
Chart row 76 1 row F.
Chart row 77 1 row J.
Chart rows 78–79 2 rows A.
Chart rows 80–158 Rep rows 1–79.
Chart rows 159–169 Rep rows 1–11.

Chart row 2 P across row, working 0 (0: 1)B, 0 (0: 2)C, 0 (1: 2)B, 0 (2: 2)C, 1 (3: 3)B, [1C, 5B, 1C, 2B, 1C, 5B, 2C, 2B, 2C, 3B] 4 times, 1C, 5B, 1C, 2B, 1C, 4 (5: 5)B, 0 (2: 2)C, 0 (1: 2)B, 0 (0: 2)C, 0 (0: 1)B.

Following stripe sequence table for background stripe colors and chart for squiggle patt in yarn C, cont in St st chart patt as set until chart row 78 has been completed *and at the same time* inc 1 st at each end of chart row 11 and every foll 4th row until there are 144 (152: 160) sts.

Shape armholes

Keeping chart patt and stripe sequence correct throughout, bind off 8 sts at beg of next 2 rows.

Dec 1 st at each end of next 7 (8: 9) rows.

Work even for 1 row.

Dec 1 st at each end of next row and 4 foll alt rows. 104 (110: 116) sts.

Work even until chart row 164 has been completed, ending with a WS row.

Shape shoulders and back neck

Bind off 10 (11: 12) sts at beg of next 2 rows.

Next row (RS) Bind off 10 (11: 12) sts, work in patt until there are 16 (17: 18) sts on right needle, then turn, leaving rem sts on a holder.

Cont on these 16 (17: 18) sts only for right side of neck.

Bind off 4 sts at beg of next row.

Bind off rem 12 (13: 14) sts.

With RS facing, rejoin yarn to rem sts and bind off center 32 sts, then work in patt to end.

Complete to match first side, reversing shapings.

left front

Using size 2 (2.75mm) needles and yarn A, cast on 56 (60: 64) sts.

Beg with a K row, work 10 rows in St st, ending with a WS row.

Next row (RS) P to end, to form fold line.

Next row P to end.

Change to size 3 (3.25mm) needles.

Beg with chart row 1 and following stripe sequence table for background stripe colors and chart for squiggle patt, work in patt foll chart between markers for left front until chart row 78 has been completed *and at the same time* inc 1 st at beg of chart row 11 and every foll 4th row until there are 72 (76: 80) sts.

Shape armhole and front neck

Keeping chart patt and stripe sequence correct throughout, bind off 8 sts at beg of next row.

Complete armhole shaping as for back (and as shown on chart) *and at the same time* shape front neck by dec 1 st at beg of next row and every foll 4th row until 32 (35: 38) sts rem.

Work even until front matches back to shoulder, ending with a WS row.

Shape shoulder

Bind off 10 (11: 12) sts at beg of next row and foll alt row.

Work even for 1 row.

Bind off rem 12 (13: 14) sts.

right front

Work as for left front, but foll chart between markers for right front and reversing shapings. Note that armhole and neck shaping begin on same row for this side of garment.

to finish

Block pieces as explained on page 141.

Sew both shoulder seams, using backstitch.

Armhole edgings

With RS facing and using size 2 (2.75mm) needle and yarn A, pick up and knit 160 (162: 164) sts evenly around armhole edge.

Row 1 (WS) P to end.

Row 2 (picot row) *K2tog, yo, rep from * to last 2 sts, K2.

Beg with a P row, work 4 rows in St st.

Bind off loosely and evenly.

Button band

With RS facing and using size 2 (2.75mm) circular needle and yarn A, pick up and knit 58 sts up right front edge from hemline fold to start of neck shaping, 68 sts up right front V-neck edge to shoulder, 40 sts across back neck edge, 68 sts down left front V-neck edge to start of neck shaping, and 58 sts down left front edge to hemline fold. 292 sts.

Row 1 (buttonhole row) (WS) P234, [yo, P2tog, P9] 5 times, yo, P2tog, P1.

Note: Mark each buttonhole position in last row with a colored thread so they can be easily identified when sewing on buttons.

Row 2 (picot row) *K2tog, yo, rep from * to last 2 sts, K2.

Beg with a P row, work 4 rows in St st *and at the same time* make 6 buttonholes on first of these rows (a WS row) to correspond with those made previously.

Bind off loosely and evenly.

Sew side seams and armhole edging seams.

Fold hem to WS along fold line and slip stitch in place.

Fold armhole edgings and button band to WS along picot row and slip stitch in place.

Press seams lightly on WS, following instructions on yarn label.

Sew on buttons to correspond with buttonholes.

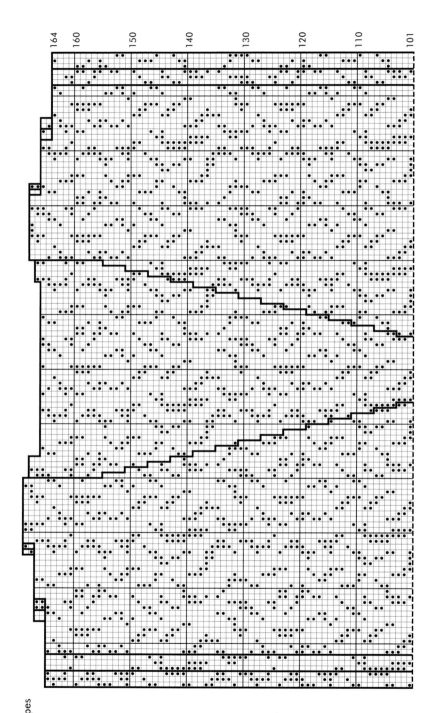

KEY

□ background stripes

● C

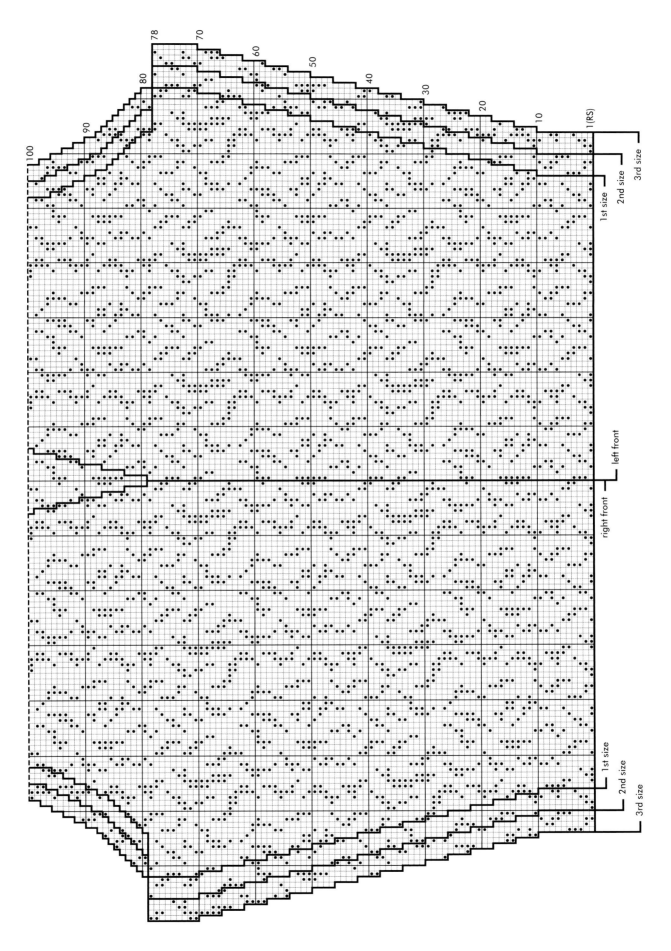

crosspatch

size and measurements

To fit chest/bust   36–38in/91–97cm
Finished knitted measurements
Around chest/bust   40in/102cm
Length to shoulder   25in/63cm
Side seam   16in/40cm

yarn

Rowan *Scottish Tweed 4-Ply* (25g/⅞oz per ball) as foll:

A	Celtic Mix 022	2 balls
B	Storm Grey 004	1 ball
C	Winter Navy 021	3 balls
D	Herring 008	1 ball
E	Grey Mist 001	2 balls
F	Midnight 023	2 balls
G	Machair 002	1 ball
H	Sea Green 006	2 balls
J	Lavender 005	1 ball

needles

Pair of size 3 (3.25mm) knitting needles, *or size to obtain correct gauge*
Pair of size 2 (2.75mm) knitting needles
Size 2 (2.75mm) circular needle 16in/40cm long for neckband

gauge

24 sts and 36 rows to 4in/10cm measured over St st chart pattern using size 3 (3.25mm) needles. *Note: To save time, take time to check gauge.*

special chart note

When reading St st chart, read all odd-numbered RS (knit) rows from right to left and all even-numbered WS (purl) rows from left to right. Use the intarsia technique, using a separate length of yarn for each area of color and twisting yarns together on WS where they meet to avoid holes.

To avoid weaving in lots of loose ends when knitting is complete, weave in ends on WS of knitting when joining in and cutting off yarns.

back

Using size 2 (2.75mm) needles and yarn C, cast on 121 sts.
Joining in and cutting off yarns as required, work in K1, P1 rib in stripes as foll:
8 rows C, 2 rows H, 1 row A, 2 rows H, and 7 rows C, inc 1 st at end of last row. 122 sts.
Change to size 3 (3.25mm) needles.
Set St st chart patt (see pages 90 and 91) on next 2 rows as foll:
Chart row 1 (RS) K to end, working 12D, 1F, 1G, 1F, 8D, 8G, 1A, 1H, 1A, 8G, 8F, 1H, 1E, 1H, 8F, 8B, 1E, 1F, 1E, 8B, 8H, 1A, 1C, 1A, 8H, 8A, 1F, 1G, 1F, 12A.
Chart row 2 P to end using same colors as previous row.
Cont in St st chart patt as set until chart row 126 has been completed, ending with a WS row.

Shape armholes

Keeping chart patt correct throughout, bind off 12 sts at beg of next 2 rows. 98 sts.
Dec 1 st at each end of next row and every foll alt row until 86 sts rem, ending with a WS row.**
Work even until chart row 210 has been completed, ending with a WS row.

Shape shoulders

Bind off 6 sts at beg of next 2 rows, then 7 sts at beg of 4 foll rows.
Bind off rem 46 sts.

front

Work as for back to **.

Divide for neck

Next row (RS) Work first 41 sts in patt, K2tog, then turn, leaving rem sts on a holder.
Cont on these 42 sts only for left side of neck.
Work even for 2 rows.
Dec 1 st at neck edge on next row and every foll alt row until 31 sts rem, then on every foll 4th row until 20 sts rem.
Work even until front matches back to shoulder, ending at armhole edge for next row.

Shape shoulder

Bind off 6 sts at beg of next row and 7 sts at beg of foll alt row.
Work even for 1 row.
Bind off rem 7 sts.
With RS facing, rejoin yarn to rem sts on holder at neck edge and K2tog, then work in patt to end. 42 sts.
Complete to match first side, reversing shapings.

to finish

Block pieces as explained on page 141.
Sew both shoulder seams, using backstitch.

Neckband

With RS facing and using size 2 (2.75mm) circular needle and yarn C, pick up and knit 82 sts down left front neck edge, 1 st at center front, 82 sts up right front neck edge, and 49 sts across back neck edge. 214 sts.
Work neckband in K1, P1 rib in rounds as foll:
Round 1 (RS) Rib to within 2 sts of center st, K2tog tbl, K1 (center st), K2tog, rib to end. 212 sts.
Work 8 rounds more in rib in same way, dec 1 st at each side of center st and working K1 for center st on every round *and at the same time* work in stripe sequence as foll:
2 rounds C, 1 round H, 1 round A, 1 round H, and 3 rounds C.
Using C, bind off in rib, dec at center front as before.

Armhole edgings

With RS facing and using size 2 (2.75mm) needles and yarn B, pick up and knit 172 sts evenly around armhole edge.
Work in K1, P1 rib in stripe sequence as foll:
2 rows B and 2 rows C.
Using yarn C, bind off loosely in rib.
Sew side and armhole edging seams.
Press seams lightly on WS, following instructions on yarn label and avoiding ribbing.

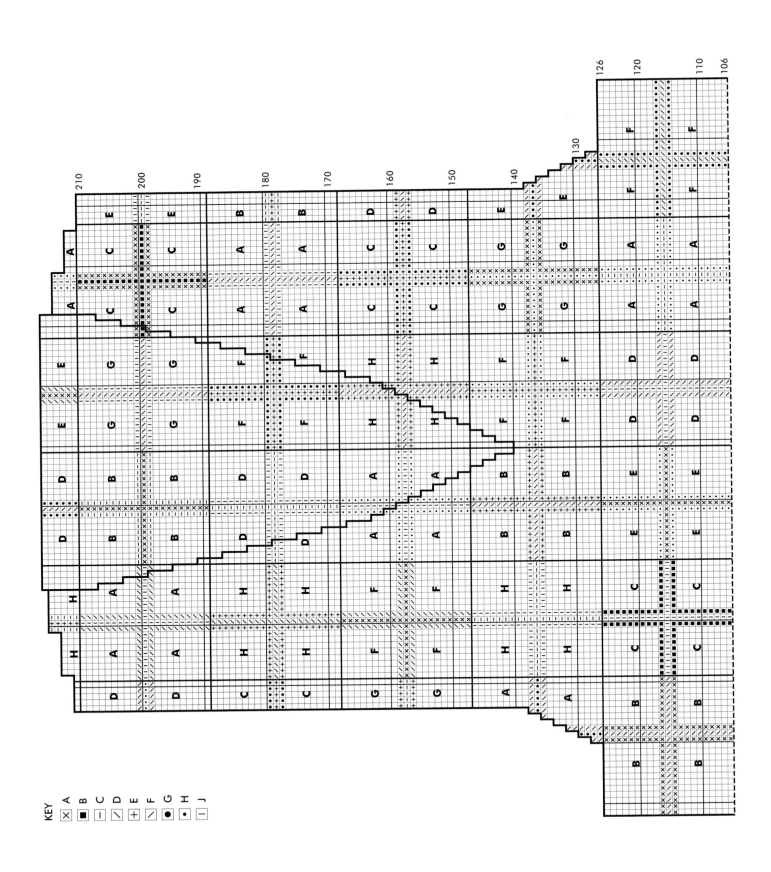

KEY A B C D E F G H J
× ■ I \ + / ● · —

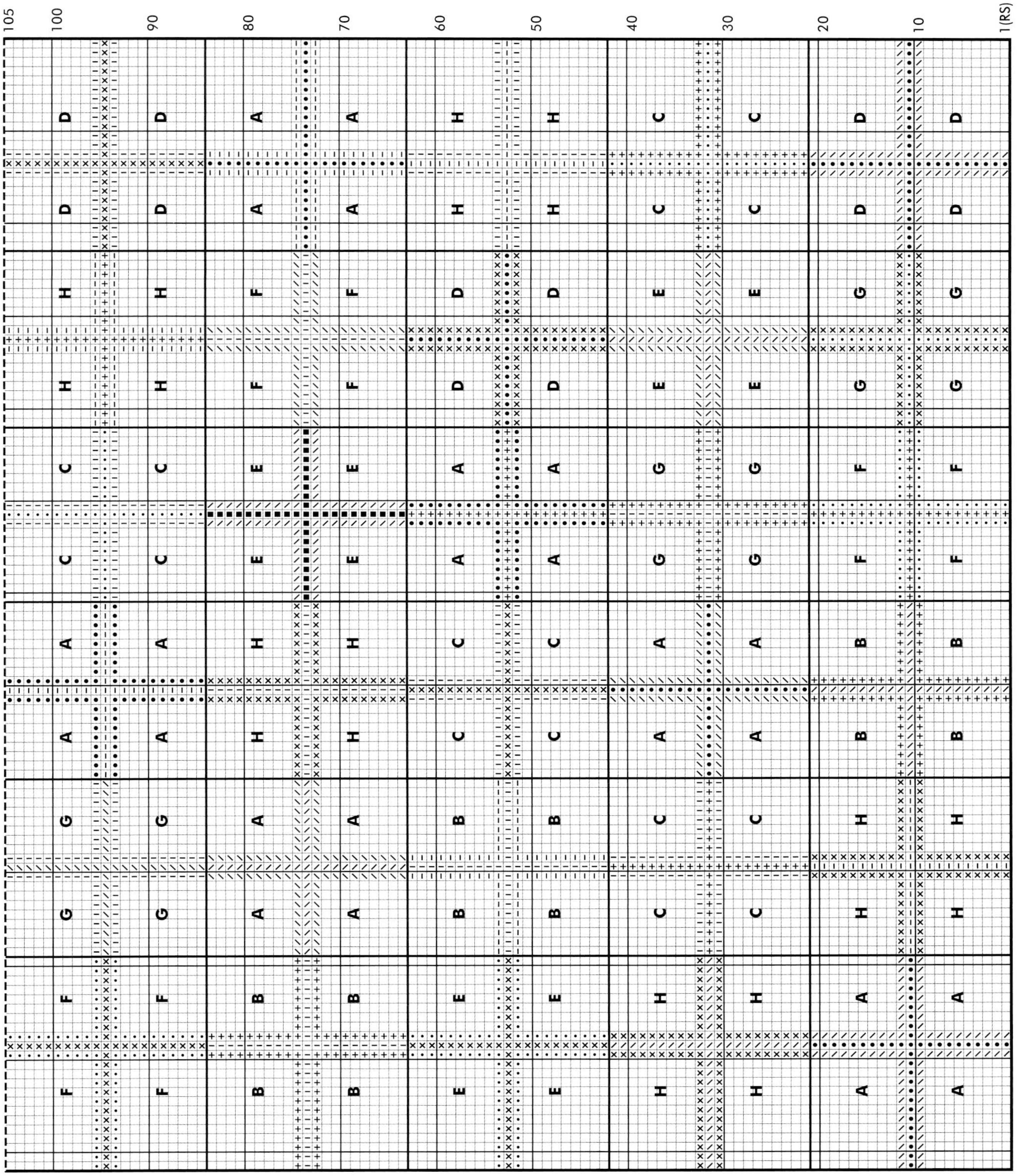
105
100
90
80
70
60
50
40
30
20
10
1(RS)

houses bag

size
Finished bag measures approximately 14in/35cm wide by
11½in/29cm tall.

yarn
Rowan *Cotton Glace* (50g/1¾oz per ball) as foll:

A	Mystic 808	3 balls
B	Nightshade 746	2 balls
C	Dijon 739	1 ball
E	Splendour 810	1 ball
F	Sky 749	1 ball
G	Spice 807	1 ball
H	Blood Orange 445	1 ball
J	Ivy 812	1 ball

Rowan *4-Ply Cotton* (50g/1¾oz per ball) as foll:

D	Nightsky 115	1 ball

needles
Pair of size 3 (3.25mm) knitting needles, *or size to obtain
correct gauge*

extras
Piece of fabric for lining, approximately 16in/40cm by
28in/70cm, and matching thread

gauge
26 sts and 36 rows to 4in/10cm measured over St st chart pattern
using size 3 (3.25mm) needles. *Note: To save time, take time to
check gauge.*

special chart note
When reading St st chart, read all odd-numbered RS (knit) rows from
right to left and all even-numbered WS (purl) rows from left to right.
Use the intarsia technique, using a separate length of yarn for each
area of color and twisting yarns together on WS where they meet to
avoid holes. But within the individual areas (for example within the
checkerboard area), use the Fair Isle technique, weaving color not in
use into back of work.
To avoid weaving in lots of loose ends when knitting is complete,
weave in ends on WS of knitting when joining in and cutting
off yarns.

front
Using size 3 (3.25mm) needles and yarn A, cast on 92 sts.
Row 1 (WS) *K1, P1, rep from * to end.
Row 2 *P1, K1, rep from * to end.
These 2 rows form seed st patt.
Work 13 rows more in seed st, ending with a WS row.
Set St st chart patt on next 2 rows as foll:
Next row (chart row 1) (RS) Using yarn A work first 10 sts in
seed st, work next 72 sts foll row 1 of chart, using yarn A work last
10 sts in seed st.
Next row (chart row 2) Using yarn A work first 10 sts in seed st,
work next 72 sts foll row 2 of chart, using yarn A work last 10 sts
in seed st.
Working first and last 10 sts in seed st using yarn A and center

72 sts in St st chart patt, cont as set until chart row 78 has been
completed, ending with a WS row.
Using yarn A only, work all sts in seed st for 10 rows.
Bind off in seed st.

back
Work exactly as for front.

strap
Using size 3 (3.25mm) needles and yarn A, cast on 17 sts.
Join in yarns H and B, and using the intarsia technique, work as foll:
Row 1 (RS) Using yarn A K9, using yarn H K4, using yarn B K4.
Row 2 Using yarn B P4, using yarn H P4, using yarn A K1, P8.

Rows 3–6 Rep rows 1–2 twice.
Row 7 Using yarn A K9, using yarn B K4, using yarn H K4.
Row 8 Using yarn H P4, using yarn B P4, using yarn A K1, P8.
Rows 9–12: Rep rows 7–8 twice.
These 12 rows form patt.
Cont in patt until strap measures approximately 64in/163cm from cast-on edge, ending with a patt row 6 (a WS row) or 12 (a WS row).
Bind off.

to finish

Block pieces as explained on page 141.
Cut two pieces of lining fabric same size as knitted front and back, adding a ½in/1.5cm seam allowance all around edge. For gussets, cut two pieces of lining fabric same width as knitted strap and same height as front/back, adding a ½in/1.5cm seam allowance all around edge.

Sew knitted strap seam to form one long narrow tube, positioning seam along one edge. Sew together knitted front and back along cast-on edges. To form gussets on bag, sew front and back to ends and folded/seamed edges of strap, matching center of end of strap to base seam and leaving approximately 41in/100cm free at center to form strap.

Sew together lining pieces as for knitted pieces (except for strap). Fold under hem at top of lining and slip stitch lining in place inside knitted bag.

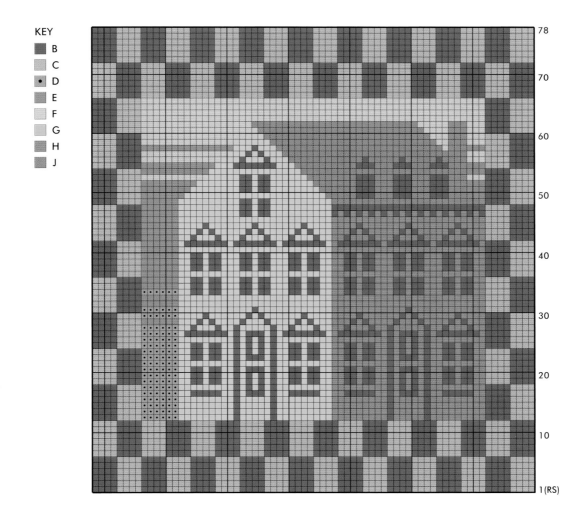

KEY
B
C
D
E
F
G
H
J

mirage

sizes and measurements

To fit chest	40–42	44	in
	97–102	112	cm

Finished knitted measurements

Around chest	47	49	in
	119	125	cm
Length to shoulder	25¾	27½	in
	66	70	cm
Sleeve seam	21½	21½	in
	54.5	54.5	cm

yarn

Rowan *Scottish Tweed 4-Ply* (25g/7/8oz per ball) as foll:

A	Thatch 018	3	3	balls
B	Mallard 020	3	4	balls
C	Midnight 023	2	2	balls
D	Sea Green 006	3	3	balls
E	Lavender 005	3	3	balls
F	Wine 012	3	3	balls
G	Celtic Mix 022	2	2	balls
H	Apple 015	2	2	balls
J	Herring 008	1	2	balls
L	Claret 013	2	2	balls
M	Thistle 016	1	2	balls
N	Winter Navy 021	1	1	ball
Q	Lobster 017	1	1	ball
R	Heath 014	2	2	balls
S	Rust 009	2	2	balls
T	Sunset 011	1	1	ball
U	Skye 003	1	1	ball
V	Machair 002	1	1	ball
W	Brilliant Pink 010	1	1	ball
X	Lewis Grey 007	1	2	balls

needles

Pair of size 2 (2.75mm) knitting needles
Pair of size 3 (3.25mm) knitting needles, *or size to obtain correct gauge*

gauge

28 sts and 34 rows to 4in/10cm measured over St st chart pattern using size 3 (3.25mm) needles. *Note: To save time, take time to check gauge.*

special chart note

When reading St st chart, read all odd-numbered RS (knit) rows from right to left and all even-numbered WS (purl) rows from left to right. Use the Fair Isle technique for background, weaving it into back of work when not in use. Use the intarsia technique for motifs, using a separate length of yarn for each area of color and twisting yarns together on WS where they meet to avoid holes.

To avoid weaving in lots of loose ends when knitting is complete, weave in ends on WS of knitting when joining in and cutting off yarns.

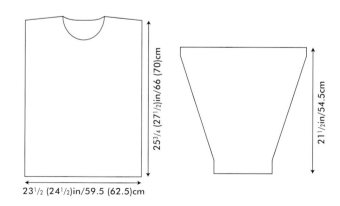

25¾ (27½)in/66 (70)cm

23½ (24½)in/59.5 (62.5)cm

21½in/54.5cm

back

Using size 2 (2.75mm) needles and yarn L, cast on 147 (155) sts.
Work 21 rows in K1, P1 rib in stripes as foll:
3 rows L, 3 rows F, 1 row A, 2 rows N, 1 row A, 2 rows S, 1 row W, 4 rows R, 2 rows E, 1 row D, and 1 row B.

Next row (inc row) (WS) Using yarn B, rib 7 (11), [M1, rib 7] 19 times, M1, rib 7 (11). 167 (175) sts.
Change to size 3 (3.25mm) needles.
Beg with a K row and chart row 15 for smallest size (chart row 1 for largest size), work chart patt in St st until chart row 216 has been completed (see pages 96 and 97), ending with a WS row.

Shape shoulders and back neck

Next row (RS) Bind off 16 (20) sts, work in patt until there are 49 sts on right needle, then turn, leaving rem sts on a holder.
Cont on these 49 sts only for right side of neck.
Keeping chart patt correct throughout, bind off 4 sts at beg of next row.
Bind off 20 sts at beg of next row.
Bind off 4 sts at beg of next row.
Bind off rem 21 sts.
With RS facing, rejoin yarn to rem sts and bind off center 37 sts, then work in patt to end.
Complete to match first side, reversing shapings.

front

Work as for back until chart row 188 has been completed, ending with a WS row.

Divide for neck

Next row (RS) Work 75 (79) sts in patt, then turn, leaving rem sts on a holder.
Cont on these 75 (79) sts only for left side of neck.
Keeping chart patt correct throughout, bind off 4 sts at beg of next row and foll alt row.
Dec 1 st at neck edge on next 6 rows and 2 foll alt rows.
Work even for 3 rows.
Dec 1 st at neck edge on next row and foll 4th row. 57 (61) sts.
Work even until front matches back to beg of shoulder shaping, ending with a WS row.

Shape left shoulder

Bind off 16 (20) sts at beg of next row and 20 sts on foll alt row.
Work even for 1 row.
Bind off rem 21 sts.
With RS facing, rejoin yarn to rem sts and bind off center 17 sts, then work in patt to end. 75 (79) sts.
Complete to match first side, reversing shapings.

sleeves (make 2)

Using size 2 (2.75mm) needles and yarn L, cast on 50 sts.
Work 21 rows in rib in stripes as for back, ending with a RS row.
Next row (inc row) (WS) Using yarn B, rib 2, [M1, rib 3] 19 times, M1, rib 2. 81 sts.
Change to size 3 (3.25mm) needles.
Beg with chart row 1, work in chart patt between markers for sleeve *and at the same time* inc 1 st at each end of chart row 3 and then on every foll 4th row until there are 151 sts.
Work even until chart row 164 has been completed.
Bind off loosely and evenly.

to finish

Block pieces as explained on page 141.
Sew right shoulder seam, using backstitch.

Neckband

With RS facing and using size 2 (2.75mm) needles and yarn L, pick up and knit 37 sts down left front neck edge, 17 sts across center front neck edge, 37 sts up right front neck edge, and 53 sts across back neck edge. 144 sts.
Work 10 rows in K1, P1 rib in stripes as foll:
2 rows L, 3 rows F, 1 row A, 2 rows N, 1 row A, 1 row S.
Using yarn S, bind off loosely and evenly in rib.
Sew left shoulder seam and neckband seam.
Sew sleeves to back and front, matching center of bound-off edge of sleeve to shoulder seam.
Sew side and sleeve seams.
Press seams lightly on WS, following instructions on yarn label and avoiding ribbing.

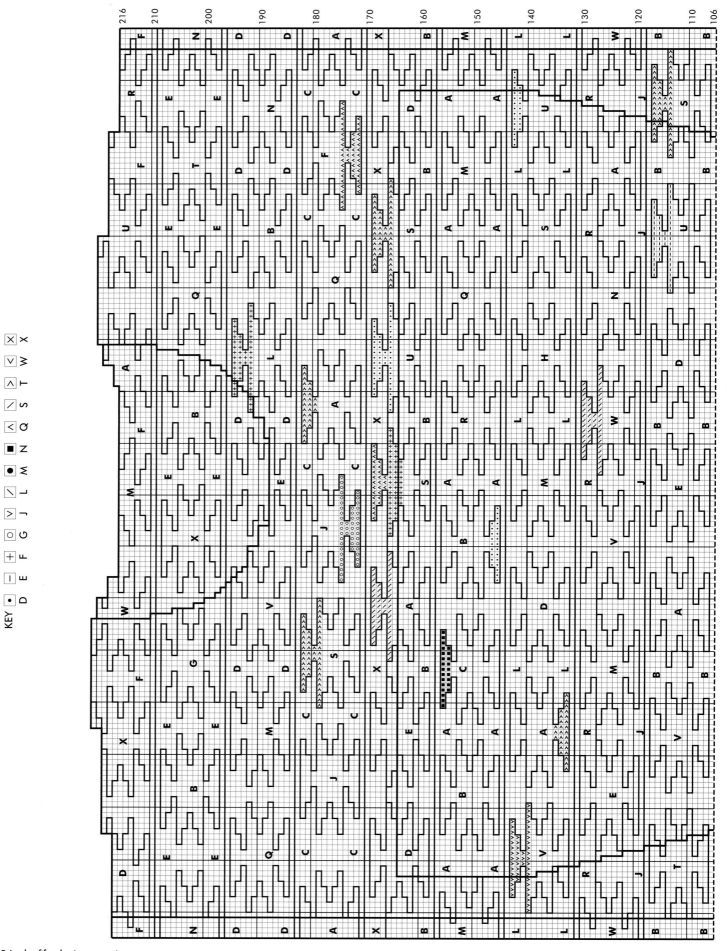

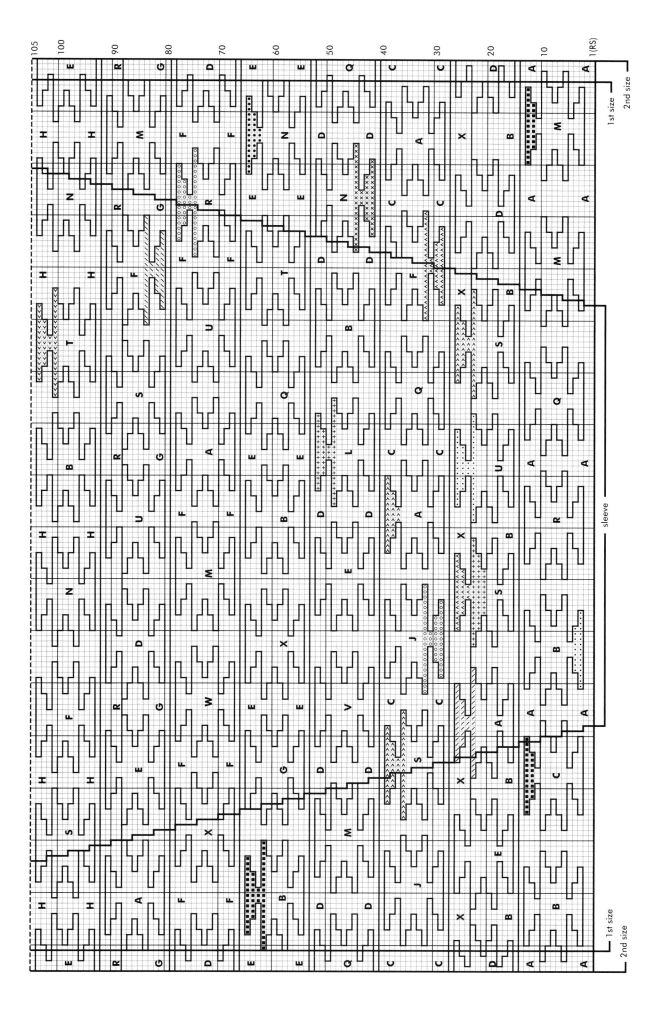

mirage 97

tumbling blocks

size and measurements

To fit chest/bust   36–38in/91–97cm

Finished knitted measurements

Around chest/bust	40in/100cm
Length to shoulder	24½in/62cm
Side seam	15¼in/38.5cm

yarn

Rowan *Scottish Tweed 4-Ply* (25g/⅞oz per ball) as foll:

A	Midnight 023	4 balls
B	Rust 009	1 ball
C	Storm Grey 004	1 ball
D	Wine 012	1 ball
E	Herring 008	1 ball
F	Claret 013	2 balls
G	Sea Green 006	1 ball
H	Lobster 017	1 ball
J	Heath 014	1 ball
L	Thatch 018	1 ball
M	Peat 019	1 ball

needles

Pair of size 3 (3.25mm) knitting needles, *or size to obtain correct gauge*
Pair of size 2 (2.75mm) knitting needles
Size 2 (3mm) circular needle 16in/40cm long for neckband

gauge

24 sts and 36 rows to 4in/10cm measured over St st chart pattern using size 3 (3.25mm) needles. *Note: To save time, take time to check gauge.*

special chart note

When reading St st chart, read all odd-numbered RS (knit) rows from right to left and all even-numbered WS (purl) rows from left to right. Use the intarsia technique, using a separate length of yarn for each area of color and twisting yarns together on WS where they meet to avoid holes.

To avoid weaving in lots of loose ends when knitting is complete, weave in ends on WS of knitting when joining in and cutting off yarns.

24½in/62cm

20in/50cm

back

Using size 2 (2.75mm) needles and yarn F, cast on 119 sts.

Using F, work 1 row in K1, P1 rib.

Cut off yarn F.

Using A, work 13 rows more in K1, P1 rib, inc 1 st at end of last row. 120 sts.

Change to size 3 (3.25mm) needles.

Set St st chart patt (see pages 100 and 101) on next 2 rows as foll:

Chart row 1 (RS) K to end, working 1A, 18B, 1C, 1A, 18D, 1E, 1A, 18F, 1G, 1A, 18H, 1J, 1A, 18L, 1C, 1A, 18F, 1E.

Chart row 2 P to end, working 2E, 16F, 2A, 2C, 16L, 2A, 2J, 16H, 2A, 2G, 16F, 2A, 2E, 16D, 2A, 2C, 16B, 2A.

Cont in St st chart patt until chart row 126 has been completed, ending with a WS row.

Shape armholes

Keeping chart patt correct throughout, bind off 12 sts at beg of each of next 2 rows, ending with a WS row. 96 sts.

Dec 1 st at each end of next row and every foll alt row until 84 sts rem.**

Work even until chart row 210 has been completed, ending with a WS row.

Shape shoulders

Bind off 6 sts at beg of each of next 2 rows, then 7 sts at beg of 4 foll rows.

Bind off rem 44 sts.

front

Work as for back to **.

Work even until chart row 146 has been completed, ending with a WS row.

Divide for neck

Next row (RS) Work first 40 sts in patt, K2tog, then turn, leaving rem sts on a holder.

Cont on these 41 sts only for left side of neck.

Work even for 2 rows.

Dec 1 st at neck edge on next row and every foll alt row until 30 sts rem, then on every foll 4th row until 20 sts rem, ending with a WS row.

Shape shoulder

Bind off 6 sts at beg of next row and 7 sts at beg of foll alt row.

Work even for 1 row.

Bind off rem 7 sts.

With RS facing, rejoin yarn to rem sts on holder and K2tog, then work in patt to end.

Complete to match first side, reversing shapings.

to finish

Block pieces as explained on page 141.

Sew both shoulder seams, using backstitch.

Neckband

With RS facing and using size 2 (2.75mm) circular needle and yarn A, pick up and knit 76 sts down left front neck edge, 1 st at center front, 76 sts up right front neck edge, and 47 sts across back neck edge. 200 sts.

Work neckband in K1, P1 rib in rounds as foll:

Round 1 (RS) Rib to within 2 sts of center st, K2tog tbl, K1 (center st), K2tog, rib to end. 198 sts.

Work 8 rounds more in rib in same way, dec 1 st at each side of center st and working K1 for center st on every round *and at the same time* use yarn A for first 7 rounds and yarn F for 8th round.

Using yarn F, bind off in rib, dec at center front as before.

Armhole edgings

With RS facing and using size 2 (2.75mm) circular needle and yarn A, pick up and knit 172 sts evenly around armhole edge.

Work 4 rows in K1, P1 rib, using yarn A for first 3 rows and yarn F for 4th row.

Using yarn F, bind off loosely in rib.

Sew side and armhole edging seams.

Press seams lightly on WS, following instructions on yarn label and avoiding ribbing.

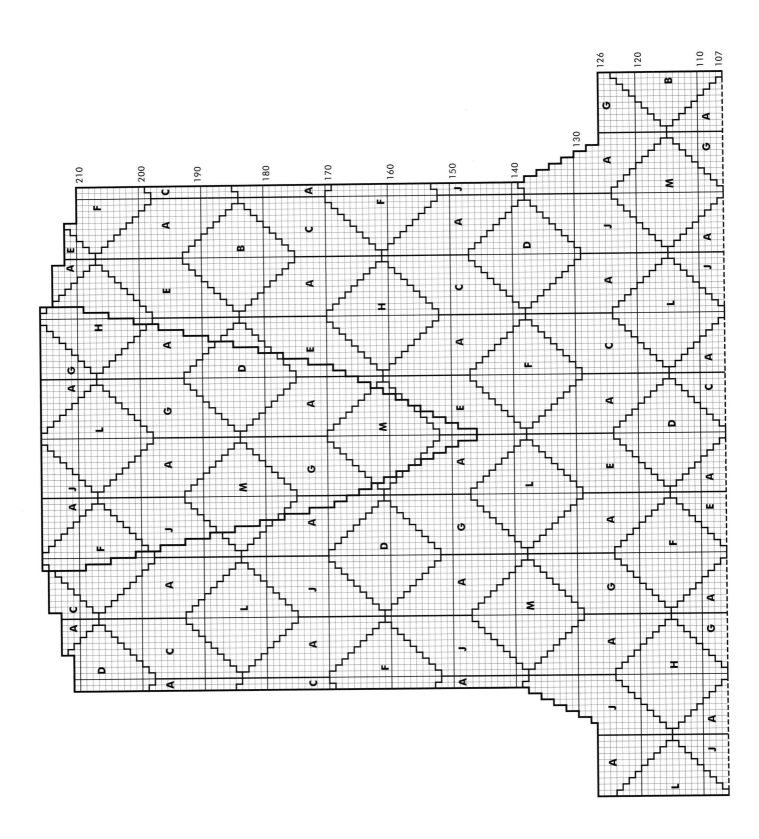

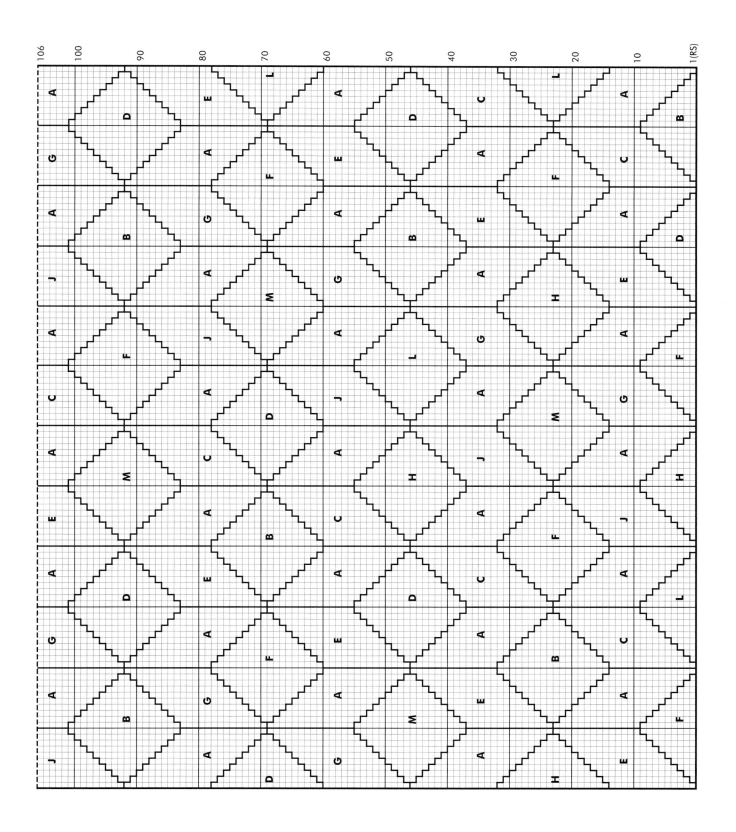

stepped flowers stole

size
Finished stole measures approximately 28½in/73cm wide by 75in/191cm long.

yarn
Rowan *Summer Tweed* (50g/1¾oz per ball) as foll:

A	Reed 514	5 balls
B	Smoulder 522	1 ball
C	Sunset 509	2 balls
D	Angel 526	2 balls
E	Exotic 512	1 ball
F	Blueberry 525	1 ball
G	Torrid 536	2 balls
H	Brilliant 528	2 balls
J	Rush 507	1 ball
K	Powder 500	1 ball
L	Choc Fudge 531	1 ball
M	Denim 529	1 ball
N	Summer Berry 537	1 ball
P	Toast 530	2 balls
R	Butter Ball 538	1 ball

needles
Pair of size 6 (4mm) knitting needles
Pair of size 8 (5mm) knitting needles, *or size to obtain correct gauge*
Size 6 (4mm) circular knitting needle

extras
2¼yd/2m of 45in/115cm-wide fabric for lining (optional)

gauge
16 sts and 23 rows to 4in/10cm measured over St st chart pattern using size 8 (5mm) needles. *Note: To save time, take time to check gauge.*

special chart note
When reading St st chart, read all odd-numbered RS (knit) rows from right to left and all even-numbered WS (purl) rows from left to right. Use the intarsia technique, using a separate length of yarn for each area of color and twisting yarns together on WS where they meet to avoid holes.
To avoid weaving in lots of loose ends when knitting is complete, weave in ends on WS of knitting when joining in and cutting off yarns.

to make stole

Using size 6 (4mm) needles and yarn P, cast on 117 sts.

Work 4 rows in garter st (K every row), ending with a WS row.

Change to size 8 (5mm) needles.

Beg with a K row and chart row 1, work in patt foll chart as foll:

Work chart rows 1–324 once (see pages 104 and 105), then rep chart rows 1–111 again, ending with a RS row.

Cut off all contrasting yarns and join in yarn P.

Change to size 6 (4mm) needles.

Next row (WS) P to end.

Rep last row twice more.

Bind off purlwise (on RS).

to finish

Block stole as explained on page 141.

Side borders

With RS facing and using size 6 (4mm) circular needle and yarn P, pick up and knit 306 sts evenly along one row-end edge.

Work 2 rows in garter st, ending with a RS row.

Bind off knitwise (on WS).

Work other side border in same way.

For lining, cut fabric to same size as knitting, adding a ½in/1.5cm seam allowance all around edge. Then fold under seam allowance all around edge of lining and sew to knitting with wrong sides together.

KEY
A
B
C
D
E
F
G
H
J
K
L
M
N
P
R

162
160

150

140

130

120

110

100

90

80

70

60

50

40

30

20

10

1(RS)

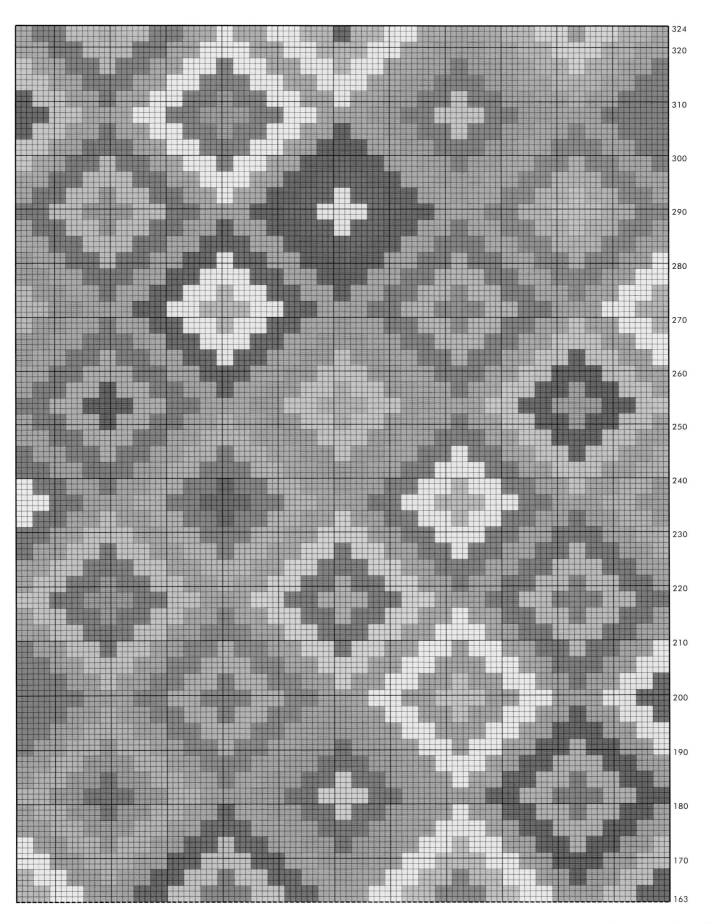

324
320
310
300
290
280
270
260
250
240
230
220
210
200
190
180
170
163

houses

size and measurements

To fit chest/bust   36–38in/91–97cm

Finished knitted measurements

Around chest/bust   43½in/111cm

Length to shoulder   24in/61cm

Side seam   15¼in/38.5cm

yarn

Rowan *Scottish Tweed 4-Ply* (25g/⅞oz per ball) as foll:

A	Thistle 016	2 balls
B	Wine 012	1 ball
C	Herring 008	1 ball
D	Lobster 017	1 ball
E	Thatch 018	1 ball
F	Heath 014	1 ball
G	Rust 009	1 ball
H	Mallard 020	1 ball
J	Claret 013	1 ball
L	Lewis Grey 007	1 ball
M	Apple 015	2 balls
N	Celtic Mix 022	1 ball
Q	Winter Navy 021	3 balls
R	Sea Green 006	1 ball
S	Midnight 023	2 balls
T	Storm Grey 004	1 ball
U	Peat 019	1 ball

needles

Pair of size 3 (3.25mm) knitting needles, *or size to obtain correct gauge*

Pair of size 2 (2.75mm) knitting needles

21¾in/55.5cm

24in/61cm

gauge

28½ sts and 31 rows to 4in/10cm measured over St st chart pattern using size 3 (3.25mm) needles. *Note: To save time, take time to check gauge.*

special chart note

When reading St st chart, read all odd-numbered RS (knit) rows from right to left and all even-numbered WS (purl) rows from left to right. The background color is used for everything that isn't a house or roof—windows, doors, stitches between houses, and single stitches between house parts and between house parts and roofs are all in the background color.

Work the background color using the Fair Isle technique, carrying it across the entire row and when it is not in use, weaving it into back of work every 3 or 4 sts.

Work the house parts and roofs with the intarsia technique, using a separate length of yarn for each area of color and twisting yarns together on WS where they meet to avoid holes.

To avoid weaving in lots of loose ends when knitting is complete, weave in ends on WS of knitting when joining in and cutting off yarns.

back

Using size 2 (2.75mm) needles and yarn U, cast on 149 sts.

Work 19 rows in K1, P1 rib in stripes as foll:

2 rows U, 2 rows A, 2 rows D, 1 row G, 4 rows C, 2 rows R, 1 row M, 3 rows U, 2 rows S.

Next row (inc row) Using S, rib 1, *work into front and back of next st to inc 1 st, rib 28, rep from * to last st, work into front and back of next st to inc 1 st, rib 2. 155 sts.

Change to size 3 (3.25mm) needles.

Using yarn Q and beg with a K row, work 4 rows in St st.

Using yarn A, work 2 rows more in St st (chart rows 1 and 2), ending with a WS row.

Set St st chart patt (see pages 108 and 109) on next 2 rows as foll:

Chart row 3 (RS) K to end, working 1A, 13B, 1A, 13C, 1A, 13D, 1A, 13E, 1A, 13F, 1A, 13G, 1A, 13H, 1A, 13J, 1A, 13L, 1A, 13E, 1A, 13M, 1A.

Chart row 5 P to end, working 1A, 13M, 1A, 13E, 1A, 13L, 1A, 13J, 1A, 13H, 1A, 13G, 1A, 13F, 1A, 13E, 1A, 13D, 1A, 13C, 1A, 13B, 1A.

Cont in St st chart patt as set until chart row 92 has been completed, ending with a WS row.

Shape armholes

Cont to foll St st chart patt throughout, bind off 14 sts at beg of each of next 2 rows. 127 sts.

Bind off 2 sts at beg of each of next 4 rows. 119 sts.

Dec 1 st at beg of each of next 6 rows, ending with a WS row. 113 sts.**

Work even until chart row 164 has been completed, ending with a WS row.

Shape shoulders

Bind off 10 sts at beg of each of next 6 rows.

Leave rem 53 sts on a holder for back neck.

front

Work as for back to **.

Divide for neck

Chart row 105 (RS) Work 54 sts in patt, K2tog, then turn, leaving rem sts on a holder.

Cont on these 55 sts only for left side of neck.

Work even for 1 row.

Dec 1 st at neck edge on next row and every foll alt row until 38 sts rem, then on every foll 3rd row until 30 sts rem.

Work even for 1 row, ending with a WS row (chart row 164).

Shape left shoulder

Bind off 10 sts at beg of next row and foll alt row.

Work even for 1 row.

Bind off rem 10 sts.

With RS facing, slip center st on holder onto a safety pin, rejoin yarn to rem sts and K2tog, then work in patt to end. 55 sts.

Work even for 1 row.

Dec 1 st at neck edge on next row and every foll alt row until 38 sts rem, then on every foll 3rd row until 30 sts rem.

Work even for 2 rows, ending with a RS row (chart row 165).

Shape right shoulder

Bind off 10 sts at beg of next row and foll alt row.

Work even for 1 row.

Bind off rem 10 sts.

to finish

Block pieces as explained on page 141.

Sew right shoulder seam, using backstitch.

Neckband

With RS facing and using size 2 (2.75mm) needles and yarn S, pick up and knit 64 sts down left front neck edge, knit center front neck st from safety pin (mark this center st with a colored thread), pick up and knit 64 sts up right front neck edge, then from back neck holder K26, K2tog, K25. 181 sts.

Work neckband in K1, P1 rib as foll:

Row 1 (WS) *P1, K1, rep from * to within 2 sts of center st, P2tog, P1 (center st), P2tog tbl, (K1, P1) to end. 179 sts.

Row 2 (RS) *K1, P1, rep from * to within 3 sts of center st, K1, P2tog tbl, K1 (center st), P2tog, K1, (P1, K1) to end. 177 sts.

Rep last 2 rows 3 times more, using yarn J for last row.

Using yarn J, bind off in rib, dec at center front as before.

Armhole edgings

Sew left shoulder seam, using backstitch, and neckband seam, using an edge-to-edge stitch.

With RS facing and using size 2 (2.75mm) needles and yarn S, pick up and knit 142 sts evenly around armhole edge.

Using yarn S, purl 1 row.

Using yarn J, knit 2 rows (the second of these 2 rows forms fold line).

Using yarn S and beg with a K row, work 4 rows in St st, ending with a WS row.

Using yarn S, bind off loosely.

Sew side and armhole edging seams, using backstitch.

Fold armhole edgings to WS along fold line and slip stitch loosely in place.

Press seams lightly on WS, following instructions on yarn label and avoiding ribbing.

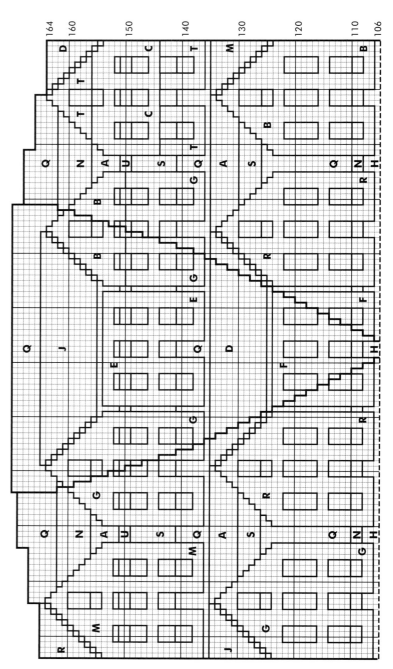

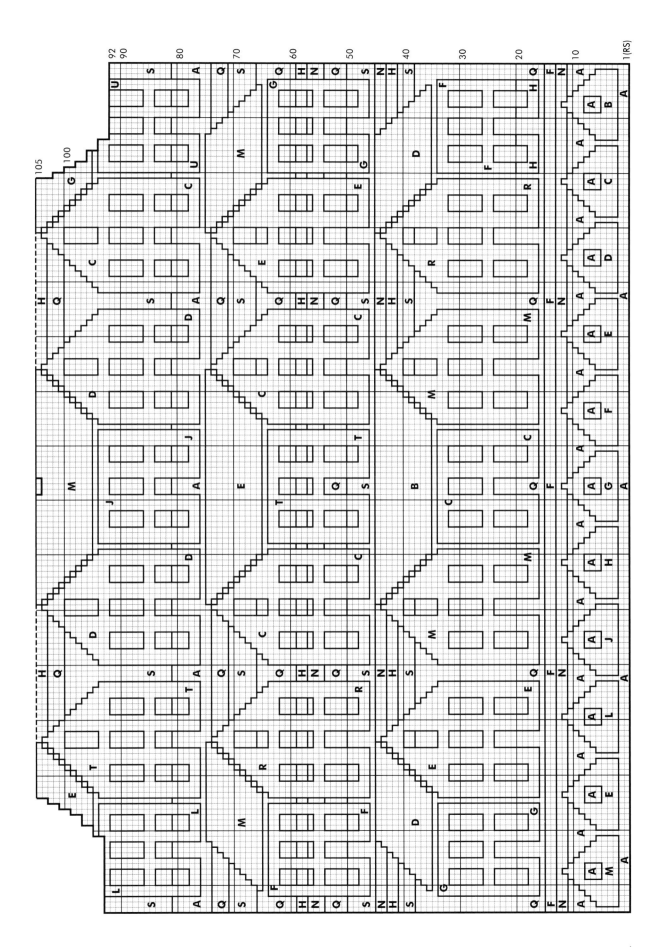

big flower throw

size
Finished chairback throw measures approximately 27½in/69cm wide by 56¾in/142cm long, including seed st border.

yarns
Rowan *Scottish Tweed Chunky* (100g/3½oz per ball) as foll:

A	Thistle 016	5 balls
B	Lobster 017	2 balls
C	Claret 013	1 balls
D	Wine 012	3 balls
E	Mallard 020	1 ball
F	Sea Green 006	1 ball

Rowan *Scottish Tweed DK* (50g/1¾oz per ball) as foll:

G	Skye 003	1 ball
H	Lavender 005	1 ball

needles
Pair of size 11 (8mm) knitting needles, *or size to obtain correct gauge*
Size 10½ (6.5mm) circular needle for border

gauge
12½ sts and 14½ rows to 4in/10cm measured over St st chart pattern using size 11 (8mm) needles and chunky yarn. *Note: To save time, take time to check gauge.*

special yarn note
Use one strand of Rowan *Scottish Tweed Chunky* yarn or two strands of Rowan *Scottish Tweed DK* yarn throughout.

special chart note
When reading St st chart, read all odd-numbered RS (knit) rows from right to left and all even-numbered WS (purl) rows from left to right. Use the intarsia technique for the flowers, using a separate length of yarn for each area of color and twisting yarns together on WS where they meet to avoid holes. But carry the background color across entire row, weaving it into the back of work when not in use. To avoid weaving in lots of loose ends when knitting is complete, weave in ends on WS of knitting when joining in and cutting off yarns.

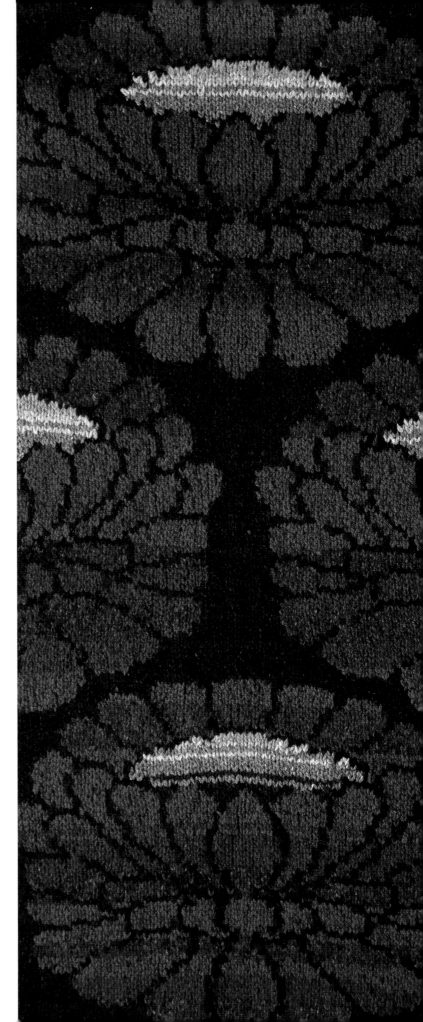

to make throw

Using size 10½ (6.5mm) circular needle and yarn A, cast on 84 sts.

Working back and forth in rows on circular needle, work border in seed st as foll:

Row 1 (dec row) (RS) K2tog, *P1, K1, rep from * to last 2 sts, P2tog. 82 sts.

Row 2 *P1, K1, rep from * to end.

Row 3 (dec row) (RS) P2tog, *K1, P1, rep from * to last 2 sts, K2tog. 80 sts.

Change to size 11 (8mm) needles.

Beg with a K row, work 2 rows in St st (these are first 2 rows of chart), ending with a WS row.

Set St st chart patt (see pages 112 and 113) on next 2 rows as foll:

Chart row 3 (RS) K39A, K2B, K39A.

Chart row 4 P38A, P4B, P38A.

Cont in St st chart patt as set, cutting off and joining in colors as required, until chart row 196 has been completed.

Top border

Change to size 10½ (6.5mm) circular needle and using yarn A only, work seed st border as foll:

Next row (RS) K to end.

**Next row (inc row) (WS) K into front and back of first st, *K1, P1, rep from * to last st, K into front and back of last st. 82 sts

Next row *P1, K1, rep from * to end.

Next row (inc row) K into front and back of first st, *P1, K1, rep from * to last st, P into front and back of last st. 84 sts.

Bind off loosely, while repeating K1, P1 to end.******

to finish

Block knitting as explained on page 141.

Side borders

Working back and forth in rows on circular needle, work seed st border along each side edge as foll:

With RS facing and using size 10½ (6.5mm) circular needle and yarn A, pick up and knit 172 sts evenly along side edge (picking up about 7 sts for every 8 rows).

Complete border as for top border from ** to **.

Sew together mitered ends of borders at corners.

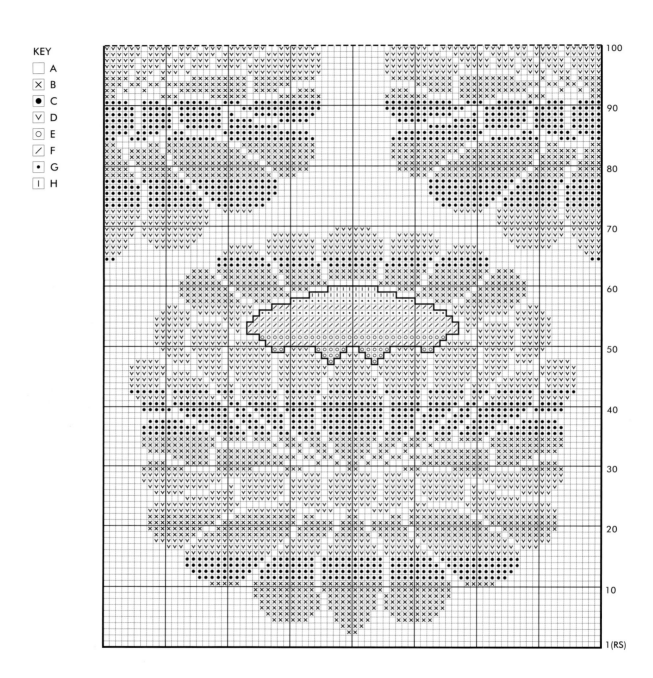

KEY

A
B ×
C ●
D ∨
E ○
F ╱
G •
H |

100
90
80
70
60
50
40
30
20
10
1(RS)

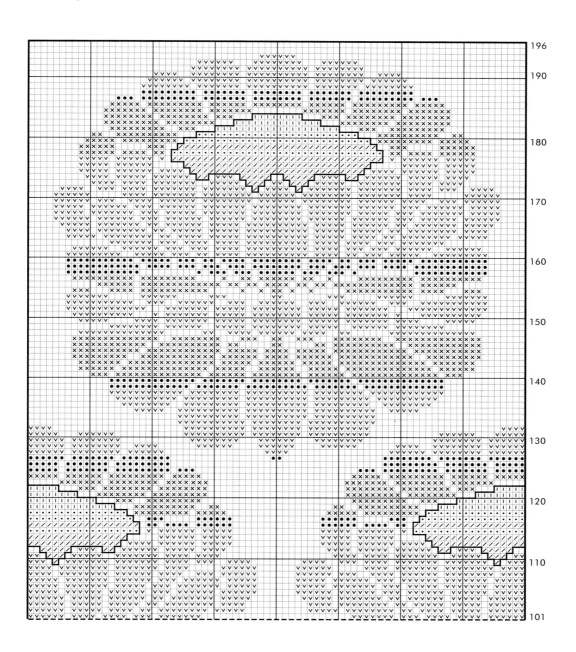

caterpillar stripes

sizes and measurements

To fit bust	32	34	36	38	40	42	in
	81	86	91	97	102	107	cm

Finished knitted measurements

Around bust	40	41	44	45½	48	50	in
	101	105	112	116	122	127	cm
Length to shoulder	21¼	21½	22	22½	22¾	23¼	in
	54	55	56	57	58	59	cm
Sleeve seam	17	17¼	17¼	17¾	17¾	18	in
	43	44	44	45	45	46	cm

yarn

Rowan *Scottish Tweed 4-Ply* (25g/⅞oz per ball) as foll:

A	Sea Green 006	2	2	2	2	2	3	balls
B	Celtic Mix 022	2	2	2	2	2	3	balls
C	Apple 015	2	2	2	2	2	3	balls
D	Winter Navy 021	2	2	2	2	2	3	balls
E	Lobster 017	2	2	2	2	2	2	balls
F	Mallard 020	2	2	2	2	2	2	balls
G	Heath 014	2	2	2	2	2	2	balls
H	Midnight 023	2	2	2	2	2	2	balls
J	Thatch 018	2	2	2	2	2	2	balls
L	Claret 013	2	2	2	2	2	2	balls
M	Rust 009	2	2	2	2	2	2	balls
N	Thistle 016	2	2	2	2	2	2	balls

needles

Pair of size 2 (2.75mm) knitting needles
Pair of size 3 (3.25mm) knitting needles, *or size to obtain correct gauge*

gauge

26 sts and 38 rows to 4in/10cm measured over St st using size 3 (3.25mm) needles. *Note: To save time, take time to check gauge.*

stripe sequence

Beg with a K row and joining in and cutting off colors as required, work stripe sequence in St st as foll:

Rows 1 and 2 Using yarn A.
Rows 3 and 4 Using yarn B.
Rows 5 to 16 Rep rows 1–4 three times.
Rows 17 and 18 Using yarn C.
Rows 19 and 20 Using yarn D.
Rows 21 to 32 Rep rows 17–20 three times.
Rows 33 and 34 Using yarn E.
Rows 35 and 36 Using yarn F.
Rows 37 to 48 Rep rows 33–36 three times.
Rows 49 and 50 Using yarn G.
Rows 51 and 52 Using yarn H.
Rows 53 to 64 Rep rows 49–52 three times.
Rows 65 and 66 Using yarn J.
Rows 67 and 68 Using yarn L.
Rows 69 to 80 Rep rows 65–68 three times.
Rows 81 and 82 Using yarn M.
Rows 83 and 84 Using yarn N.
Rows 85 to 96 Rep rows 81–84 three times.
These 96 rows form the stripe sequence and are repeated.

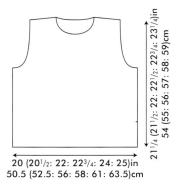

21¼ (21½: 22: 22½: 22¾: 23¼)in
54 (55: 56: 57: 58: 59)cm

20 (20½: 22: 22¾: 24: 25)in
50.5 (52.5: 56: 58: 61: 63.5)cm

17 (17¼: 17¼: 17¾: 17¾: 18)in
43 (44: 44: 45: 45: 46)cm

back

Using size 2 (2.75mm) needles and yarn D, cast on 131 (137: 145: 151: 159: 165) sts.
Work in garter st (K every row) for 6 rows, ending with a WS row.
Change to size 3 (3.25mm) needles.
Beg with a K row and row 1, work in St st in stripe sequence (see above) until back measures 13 (13¼: 13¼: 13¾: 13¾: 14)in/ 33 (34: 34: 35: 35: 36)cm from cast-on edge, ending with a WS row.

Shape armholes

Keeping stripes correct throughout, bind off 5 (6: 6: 7: 7: 8) sts at beg of next 2 rows. 121 (125: 133: 137: 145: 149) sts.
Dec 1 st at each end of next 7 (7: 9: 9: 11: 11) rows, then on foll

5 (6: 7: 8: 9: 10) alt rows. 97 (99: 101: 103: 105: 107) sts.
Work even until armhole measures 8¼ (8¼: 8½: 8½: 9: 9)in/
21 (21: 22: 22: 23: 23)cm, ending with a WS row.

Shape shoulders and back neck
Bind off 10 (10: 10: 10: 10: 11) sts at beg of next 2 rows.
77 (79: 81: 83: 85: 85) sts.
Next row (RS) Bind off 10 (10: 10: 10: 10: 11) sts, K until there
are 13 (13: 14: 14: 15: 14) sts on right needle, then turn, leaving
rem sts on a holder.
Work each side of neck separately.
Bind off 4 sts at beg of next row.
Bind off rem 9 (9: 10: 10: 11: 10) sts.
With RS facing, rejoin appropriate yarn to rem sts and bind off
center 31 (33: 33: 35: 35: 35) sts, then K to end.
Complete to match first side, reversing shapings.

front
Work as for back until 22 (22: 22: 24: 24: 24) rows less have
been worked than on back to beg of shoulder shaping, ending with
a WS row.

Shape neck
Next row (RS) K40 (40: 41: 42: 43: 44), then turn, leaving rem
sts on a holder.
Work each side of neck separately.
Keeping stripes correct throughout, dec 1 st at neck edge of next
6 rows, then on foll 4 (4: 4: 5: 5: 5) alt rows, then on foll 4th row.
29 (29: 30: 30: 31: 32) sts.
Work 3 rows, ending with a WS row.

Shape shoulder
Bind off 10 (10: 10: 10: 10: 11) sts at beg of next and foll alt row.
Work 1 row.

Bind off rem 9 (9: 10: 10: 11: 10) sts.
With RS facing, rejoin appropriate yarn to rem sts and bind off
center 17 (19: 19: 19: 19: 19) sts, then K to end.
Complete to match first side, reversing shapings.

sleeves (make 2)
Using size 2 (2.75mm) needles and yarn D, cast on 57 (57: 59:
61: 61: 63) sts.
Work in garter st for 6 rows, ending with a WS row.
Change to size 3 (3.25mm) needles.
Beg with a K row, work 6 rows in St st in stripes as foll:
2 rows yarn H, 2 rows yarn G, and 2 rows yarn H.
Cont in St st and beg with **row 65**, work in St st in stripe sequence
and at the same time shape sides by inc 1 st at each end of next
row and every foll 8th row until there are 73 (79: 81: 79: 89: 87)
sts, then on every foll 10th row until there are 89 (91: 93: 95: 97:
99) sts.
Work even until sleeve measures approximately 17 (17¼: 17¼:
17¾: 17¾: 18)in/43 (44: 44: 45: 45: 46)cm, ending after
same stripe row as on back to beg of armhole shaping and with
a WS row.
Shape top of sleeve
Keeping stripes correct, bind off 5 (6: 6: 7: 7: 8) sts at beg of next
2 rows. 79 (79: 81: 81: 83: 83) sts.
Dec 1 st at each end of next 5 rows, then on foll 3 alt rows, then
on every foll 4th row until 55 (55: 57: 57: 59: 59) sts rem.
Work 1 row.
Dec 1 st at each end of next row and every foll alt row until 39 sts
rem, then on foll 5 rows, ending with a WS row.
Bind off rem 29 sts.

to finish
Block pieces as explained on page 141.
Sew right shoulder seam, using backstitch.
Collar
With RS facing and using size 3 (3.25mm) needles and yarn A,
pick up and knit 26 (26: 26: 28: 28: 28) sts down left front neck
edge, 17 (19: 19: 19: 19: 19) sts across center front neck edge,
26 (26: 26: 28: 28: 28) sts up right front neck edge, and 39 (41:
41: 43: 43: 43) sts across back neck edge. 108 (112: 112:
118: 118: 118) sts.
Beg with row 1 of stripe patt and a K row (so that WS of body
becomes RS of collar), work in St st in stripe sequence (see beg of
instructions) for 62 rows, ending with a WS row.
Cut off contrasting yarns and change to yarn D.
Work in garter st for 5 rows, ending with a RS row.
Bind off knitwise (on WS).
Sew left shoulder and collar seam, reversing collar seam for
turn-back.
Sew side seams. Sew sleeve seams, then set in sleeves, matching
center of top of sleeve to shoulder seam.
Press seams lightly on WS, following instructions on yarn label.

crisscross

sizes and measurements

To fit chest 40–46in/102–117cm

Finished knitted measurements

Around chest   51½in/128cm
Length to shoulder   26¼in/66cm
Sleeve seam   20in/50.5cm

yarn

Rowan *Scottish Tweed 4-Ply* (25g/⅞oz per ball) as foll:

A	Grey Mist 001	11 balls
B	Midnight 023	11 balls
C	Lewis Grey 007	2 balls
D	Herring 008	2 balls
E	Heath 014	2 balls
F	Storm Grey 004	2 balls

needles

Pair of size 3 (3.25mm) knitting needles
Pair of size 5 (3.75mm) knitting needles, *or size to obtain correct gauge*

gauge

28 sts and 32 rows to 4in/10cm measured over St st chart pattern using size 5 (3.75mm) needles. *Note: To save time, take time to check gauge.*

special size note

This is a loose-fitting design. Note the width of the garment and sleeve length before beginning and match these measurements to an existing garment to get an idea of the how the finished garment will fit.

The chart design would also make a good cushion cover. For a cushion cover measuring approximately 17in/43cm square, follow the first 122 stitches of the chart and work to row 138.

special chart note

When reading St st chart, read all odd-numbered RS (knit) rows from right to left and all even-numbered WS (purl) rows from left to right. Use a separate length of yarn for each area of color, using the intarsia technique—EXCEPT for individual squares. Work across individual squares with yarns A and B using the Fair Isle technique, weaving color not in use into back of work. When using the intarsia technique, twist yarns together on WS where they meet to avoid holes.

To avoid weaving in lots of loose ends when knitting is complete, weave in ends on WS of knitting when joining in and cutting off yarns.

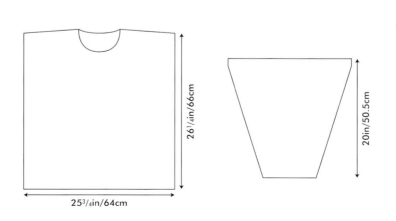

back

Using size 3 (3.25mm) needles and yarn B, cast on 150 sts.
Work rib as foll:

Rib row 1 (RS) Using yarn B, *K2, P2, rep from * to last
2 sts, K2.

Rib row 2 Using yarn B, *P2, K2, rep from * to last 2 sts, P2.

Rib row 3 Using yarn A, rep row 1.

Rib row 4 Using yarn A, rep row 2.

Rib rows 5–20 Rep rows 1–4 four times.

Rib rows 21–23 Rep rows 1–3.

Rib row 24 (inc row) (WS) Using yarn A, rib 3, [M1, rib 5] 29
times, M1, rib 2. 180 sts.

Change to size 5 (3.75mm) needles.

Using yarn C and beg with a K row, work 2 rows in St st (these are
first 2 rows on chart), ending with a WS row.

Set St st chart patt (see pages 118 and 119) on next 2 rows as foll:

Chart row 3 (RS) K across row, working 3F, 2B, 3A, 3B, 9A, 3B,
6A, 3D, 3B, 4A, 11C, 4A, 2B, 4C, 1B, 2A, 3B, 1A, 3B, 2A, 3B,
1A, 3B, 6A, 2B, 4F, 17B, 6A, 3B, 4E, 3B, 10A, 3B, 8A, 2B, 1A,
4D, 2B, 3A, 3B, 9A, 3B, 6A, 2C.

Chart row 4 P across row, working 2C, 2B, 5A, 3B, 7A, 3B, 4A,
2B, 4D, 1A, 3B, 7A, 3B, 10A, 3B, 4E, 3B, 6A, 17B, 4F, 3B, 6A,
5B, 4A, 5B, 3A, 1B, 4C, 2B, 7A, 3B, 8A, 3B, 1A, 3D, 2B, 5A,
3B, 7A, 3B, 4A, 2B, 3F.

Cont in St st chart patt as set until chart row 190 has been
completed, ending with a WS row.

Shape shoulders and back neck

Next row (RS) Bind off 23 sts, work in patt until there are 49 sts
on right needle, then turn, leaving rem sts on a holder.

Cont on these 49 sts only for right side of neck.

Keeping chart patt correct throughout, bind off 2 sts at beg of
next row.

Next row (RS) Bind off 22 sts, work in patt to last 2 sts, K2tog.

Bind off 2 sts at beg of next row.

Bind off rem 22 sts.

With RS facing, rejoin yarn to rem sts and bind off center 36 sts,
then work in patt to end.

Complete to match first side, reversing shapings.

front

Work as for back until chart row 164 has been completed, ending
with a WS row.

Divide for neck

Next row (RS) Work 82 sts in patt, then turn, leaving rem sts on
a holder.

Cont on these 82 sts only for left side of neck.

Keeping chart patt correct throughout, bind off 4 sts at beg of
next row.

Dec 1 st at neck edge on next 7 rows, 2 foll alt rows, and then

2 foll 4th rows. 67 sts.

Work even until chart row 190 has been completed, ending with a
WS row.

Shape left shoulder

Bind off 23 sts at beg of next row.

Work even for 1 row.

Bind off 22 sts at beg of next row.

Work even for 1 row.

Bind off rem 22 sts.

With RS facing, rejoin yarn to rem sts and bind off center 16 sts,
then work in patt to end. 82 sts.

Complete to match first side, reversing shapings.

sleeves (make 2)

Using size 3 (3.25mm) needles and yarn B, cast on 50 sts.

Work 23 rows in rib as for back, ending with a RS row.

Rib row 24 (inc row) (WS) Using yarn A, rib 4, [M1, rib 2, M1,
rib 3] 9 times, rib 1. 68 sts.

Change to size 5 (3.75mm) needles.

Beg with chart row 1, work in chart patt between markers for sleeve
and at the same time inc 1 st at each end of every 3rd row until
there are 98 sts, and then on every foll 4th row until there are
142 sts.

Work even until chart row 140 has been completed.

Bind off loosely and evenly.

to finish

Block pieces as explained on page 141.

Sew right shoulder seam, using backstitch.

Neckband

With RS facing and using size 3 (3.25mm) needles and yarn A,
pick up and knit 26 sts down left front neck edge, 16 sts across
center front neck edge, 26 sts up right front neck edge, and 46 sts
across back neck edge. 114 sts.

Work rib as foll:

Rib row 1 (WS) Using yarn A, *P2, K2, rep from * to last 2 sts,
P2.

Rib row 1 Using yarn A, *K2, P2, rep from * to last 2 sts, K2.

Rib row 3 Using yarn B, rep row 1.

Rib row 4 Using yarn B, rep row 2.

Rep rib rows 1–4 once more.

Using yarn B, bind off loosely and evenly in rib.

Sew left shoulder seam and neckband seam.

Sew sleeves to back and front, matching center of bound-off edge of
sleeve to shoulder seam.

Sew side and sleeve seams.

Press seams lightly on WS, following instructions on yarn label and
avoiding ribbing.

jack's back

sizes and measurements

To fit bust/chest	34	36–38	in
	86	91–97	cm

Finished knitted measurements

Around bust/chest	38	42	in
	96	106	cm
Length to shoulder	25½	26½	in
	65	68	cm
Sleeve seam	18	19	in
	46	45	cm

yarn

Rowan *Scottish Tweed 4-Ply* (25g/⅞oz per ball) as foll:

A	Lavender 005	3	3	balls
B	Herring 008	5	5	balls
D	Storm Grey 004	3	4	balls
E	Celtic Mix 022	4	4	balls
F	Skye 003	3	3	balls
G	Machair 002	3	3	balls
H	Grey Mist 001	1	2	balls
J	Lewis Grey 007	4	5	balls
L	Apple 015	1	2	balls
M	Mallard 020	2	3	balls
N	Winter Navy 021	2	2	balls
Q	Rust 009	1	2	balls

Rowan *Scottish Tweed DK* (50g/1¾oz per ball) as foll:

Y	Peat 019	2	2	balls

needles

Pair of size 7 (4.5mm) knitting needles
Pair of size 8 (5mm) knitting needles, *or size to obtain correct gauge*

gauge

18 sts and 23 rows to 4in/10cm measured over St st chart pattern using size 8 (5mm) needles and two strands of 4-ply yarn. *Note: To save time, take time to check gauge.*

special yarn note

All 4-ply yarns are used double. For example, "AB" means one strand each of yarns A and B held together. Only yarn Y (a double-knitting-weight yarn) is used single.

Only two mixed colors (for example, AB and BD) are used in each row. Refer to the color sequence table lists for which two mixed colors to use in each rows.

special chart note

When reading St st chart, read all odd-numbered RS (knit) rows from right to left and all even-numbered WS (purl) rows from left to right. Use the Fair Isle technique, weaving colors not in use into back of work.

To avoid weaving in lots of loose ends when knitting is complete, weave in ends on WS of knitting when joining in and cutting off yarns.

25½ (26½)in/65 (68)cm

19 (21)in/48 (53)cm

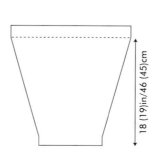

18 (19)in/46 (45)cm

color sequence table

After completing these 100 rows, begin again from row 1.

Chart rows	□	☒
1–2	AB	BD
3	AB	JJ
4	AB	Y
5	AB	BE
6–7	BB	BE
8	BB	Y
9–12	BF	Y
13	AB	Y
14	AB	EE
15	BG	EE
16	BG	JJ
17–19	GH	JJ
20	GH	JL
21–22	GH	EJ
23	FG	EJ
24–25	FG	EM
26	BF	EM
27–29	BF	MM
30	BD	MM
31–33	BD	JN
34	DD	JN
35	DD	EN
36	JJ	EN
37–38	BF	EN
39–40	BF	Y
41–42	AA	EM
43–44	AQ	EM
45–50	AD	JN
51	AF	NN

Chart rows	□	☒
52–54	BF	NN
55–56	BH	EN
57–58	BH	EL
59	BH	LM
60	BH	JM
61	BH	Y
62	BH	MM
63–64	BH	JM
65	BH	JJ
66–70	DG	JJ
71	DG	Y
72	DF	Y
73–76	DG	Y
77–78	GH	Y
79–80	GH	EJ
81	QQ	EJ
82–83	QQ	EE
84	QQ	EN
85	AD	BM
86	AD	Y
87	AQ	Y
88	AF	Y
89	AH	Y
90	AF	Y
91–94	DF	JJ
95	FG	JJ
96–99	FG	EJ
100	FG	BD

back

Using size 7 (4.5mm) needles and yarn BL, cast on 81 (89) sts.
Work 15 rows in K1, P1 rib in stripes as foll:
1 row BL, 4 rows JM, 2 rows Y, 1 row BB, 2 rows FJ, 1 row BB, 1 row Y, 3 rows JM.

Smallest size only
Next row (inc row) Using JM, *work into front and back of next st to inc 1 st, rib 7, rep from * to last st, rib 1. 91 sts.

Largest size only
Next row (inc row) Using JM, *work into front and back of next st to inc 1 st, rib 7, rep from * to last st, work into front and back of last st to inc 1 st. (101 sts)

Both sizes
Change to size 8 (5mm) needles.

Set St st chart patt (see page 122) on next 2 rows as foll:
Chart row 1 (RS) K across row, working 9 (2) BD, [1 AB, 23 BD] 3 (4) times, 1 AB, 9 (2) BD.
Chart row 2 P across row, working 8 (1) BD, 2 AB, [1 AB, 21 BD, 2 AB] 3 (4) times, 1 AB, 8 (1) BD.
Cont in St st chart patt as set, rep chart rows 1–20 until 78 chart patt rows have been completed *and at the same time* foll color sequence table for colors, ending with a WS row.

Shape armholes
Foll color sequence table and keeping chart patt correct as set throughout, bind off 10 sts at beg of each of next 2 rows, ending with a WS row. 71 (81) sts.**
Work even until 130 (136) chart patt rows in all have been worked, ending with a WS row.

Shape right shoulder and back neck
Next row (RS) Bind off 6 (8) sts, work in patt until there are 21 (24) sts on right needle, then turn, leaving rem sts on a holder.
Cont on these 21 (24) sts only for right side of neck.
Bind off 5 sts at beg of next row and 6 (8) sts at beg of foll row. 10 (11) sts.
Work even for 1 row.
Bind off 4 sts at beg of next row.
Bind off rem 6 (7) sts.

Shape left shoulder
With RS facing, rejoin yarn to rem sts on holder at neck edge and bind off 17 sts for center back neck, then work in patt to end. 27 (32) sts.
Next row (WS) Bind off 6 (8) sts, work in patt to end. 21 (24) sts.
Bind off 5 sts at beg of next row and 6 (8) sts at beg of foll row. 10 (11) sts.
Work even for 1 row.
Bind off 4 sts at beg of next row.
Bind off rem 6 (7) sts.

front
Work as for back to **.

Divide for neck
Next row (RS) Work 33 (38) sts in patt, K2tog, then turn, leaving rem sts on a holder.
Cont on these 34 (39) sts only for left side of neck.
Dec 1 st at neck edge on every foll 3rd row until 18 (23) sts rem.
Work even until 130 (136) chart patt rows in all have been worked, ending with a WS row.

Shape left shoulder
Bind off 6 (8) sts at beg of next row and foll alt row. 6 (7) sts.
Work even for 1 row.
Bind off.
With RS facing, slip center st on spare needle onto a safety pin, then rejoin yarn to rem sts, K2tog, work in patt to end. 34 (39) sts.
Dec 1 st at neck edge on every foll 3rd row until 18 (23) sts rem.
Work even until 131 (137) chart patt rows in all have been worked, ending with a RS row.

Shape right shoulder

Bind off 6 (8) sts at beg of next row and foll alt row. 6 (7) sts.
Work even for 1 row.
Bind off.

sleeves (make 2)

Using size 7 (4.5mm) needles and yarn BL, cast on 41 (43) sts.
Work 15 rows in K1, P1 rib in stripes as for back.
Next row (inc row) Using JM, rib 1 (3), *work into front and back
of next st to inc 1 st, rib 4, rep from * to end. 49 (51) sts.
Change to size 8 (5mm) needles and beg color patt from chart and
color sequence table, working between sleeve markers *and at the
same time* inc 1 st at each end of every foll 4th row until there are
89 (99) sts.
Cont to foll color sequence table and chart patt as set, work even
until 100 (106) chart rows have been completed.
Bind off.

to finish

Block pieces as explained on page 141.
Sew right shoulder seam, using backstitch.

Neckband

With RS facing and using size 7 (4.5mm) needles and yarn BB,
pick up and knit 50 (56) sts down left front neck edge, knit center
front neck st from safety pin, pick up and knit 50 (56) sts up right
front neck edge and 42 sts across back neck edge. 143 (155) sts.
Cut off yarn BB.
Work neckband in K1, P1 rib as foll:
Row 1 (WS) Using Y, rib to within 2 sts of center st, P2tog tbl, P1
(center st), P2tog, rib to end. 141 (153) sts.
Cut off yarn Y.
Row 2 (RS) Using yarn JM, rib to within 2 sts of center st, K2tog
tbl, K1 (center st), K2tog, rib to end. 139 (151) sts.
Rep last 2 rows twice more *and at the same time* work 4 rows in
stripes as foll:
3 rows JM and 1 row BL.
Next row (WS) Using BL, rib to within 2 sts of center st, P2tog tbl,
P1, P2tog, rib to end.
Using BL, bind off in rib and while binding off work dec at each
side of center st as before.
Sew left shoulder seam, using backstitch.
Sew sleeves to armholes, matching center of bound-off edge of
sleeve to shoulder seam and sewing bound-off edge of sleeve top to
straight vertical edge of armhole and approximately last 2in/5cm of
side edge of sleeve to 10 bound-off sts at underarm.
Sew side and sleeve seams.
Press seams lightly on WS, following instructions on yarn label and
avoiding ribbing.

KEY
☐ See Table on page 121
☒ for yarns

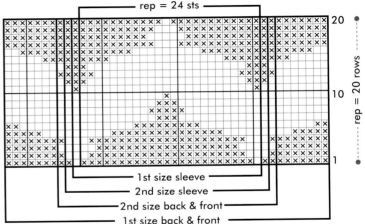

tulips

size and measurements

To fit bust   36–38in/91–97cm

Finished knitted measurements

Around bust   41½in/105cm
Length to shoulder 20¾in/52.5cm
Sleeve seam   17in/43cm

yarn

Rowan *Handknit Cotton* (50g/1¾oz per ball) as foll:

A	Tope 253	9 balls
B	Spanish Red 307	1 ball
C	Slippery 316	4 balls
D	Rosso 215	1 ball
E	Ice Water 239	1 ball
F	Diana 287	1 ball
G	Sugar 303	1 ball
H	Lupin 305	1 ball
J	Gooseberry 219	1 ball

needles

Pair of size 5 (3.75mm) knitting needles
Pair of size 6 (4mm) knitting needles, *or size to obtain correct gauge*

gauge

20 sts and 26 rows to 4in/10cm measured over St st chart pattern using size 6 (4mm) needles. *Note: To save time, take time to check gauge.*

special chart note

When reading St st chart, read all odd-numbered RS (knit) rows from right to left and all even-numbered WS (purl) rows from left to right. Use intarsia technique, using a separate length of yarn for each area of color and twisting yarns together on WS where they meet to avoid holes.

To avoid weaving in lots of loose ends when knitting is complete, weave in ends on WS of knitting when joining in and cutting off yarns.

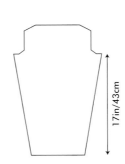

20¾in/52.5cm

20¾in/52.5cm

17in/43cm

back

Using size 5 (3.75mm) needles and yarn B, cast on 88 sts.
Work 13 rows in K1, P1 rib in stripes as foll:
2 rows A, 1 row C, 2 rows A, 1 row D, 2 rows A, 1 row E,
2 rows A, 1 row F, and 1 row A.
Next row (inc row) (WS) Using yarn A, rib 4, [M1, rib 5] 16 times, M1, rib 4. 105 sts.
Change to size 6 (4mm) needles.
Set St st chart patt on next 2 rows as foll:
Chart row 1 (RS) K across row, working 1A, 4C, 2A, 2C, 3A, 3C, 7A, 2C, 3A, 1C, 3A, 1D, 1G, 2D, 3G, [2D, 1G] twice, 3A, 3C, 11A, 3C, 3A, 2C, 2A, [3C, 1A] twice, 2C, 9A, 3C, 12A.
Chart row 2 P across row, working 11A, 3C, 10A, 2C, 1A, 2C, 2A, 3C, 2A, 2C, 3A, 3C, 10A, 3C, 3A, 1G, 2D, 2G, 1D, 5G, 1D, 1G, 1D, 3A, 1C, 2A, 4C, 6A, 3C, 4A, 2C, 2A, 3C, 1A.
Cont in St st chart patt as set until chart row 76 has been completed, ending with a WS row.

Shape armholes

Keeping chart patt correct throughout, bind off 6 sts at beg of next 2 rows.
Dec 1 st at each end of next row and every foll alt row until there are 67 sts.
Work even for 23 rows, ending with a WS row (chart row 126).

Shape shoulders

Next row (RS) Bind off 6 sts, work in patt until there are 19 sts on right needle, then turn, leaving rem sts on a holder.
Cont on these 19 sts only for right side of neck.
Bind off 5 sts at beg of next row.
Bind off 6 sts at beg of next row.
Bind off 3 sts at beg of next row.
Bind off rem 5 sts.
With RS facing, rejoin yarn to rem sts and bind off center 17 sts, then work in patt to end.
Complete to match first side, reversing shapings.

front

Work as for back until chart row 102 has been completed, ending with a WS row. (There are 69 sts rem after chart row 102 has been completed).

Divide for neck

Next row (RS) K2tog, work 28 sts in patt, then turn, leaving rem sts on a holder.
Cont on these 29 sts only for left side of neck.
Keeping chart patt correct throughout, bind off 3 sts at beg of next row and foll alt row.
Dec 1 st at neck edge on next 6 rows. 17 sts.

Work even for 14 rows, ending with a WS row.

Shape left shoulder

Bind off 6 sts at beg of next row and foll alt row.
Work even for 1 row.
Bind off rem 5 sts.
With RS facing, rejoin yarn to rem sts and bind off center 9 sts, then work in patt to last 2 sts, K2tog. 29 sts.
Complete to match first side, reversing shapings.

sleeves (make 2)

Using size 5 (3.75mm) needles and yarn B, cast on 44 sts.
Work 13 rows in rib in stripes as for back, ending with a RS row.
Next row (inc row) (WS) Using yarn A, rib 2, [M1, rib 5] 8 times, M1, rib 2. 53 sts.
Change to size 6 (4mm) needles.
Beg with chart row 1, work in chart patt between markers for sleeve until chart row 100 has been completed *and at the same time* inc 1 st at each end of chart row 7 and then on every foll 7th row until there are 79 sts.

Shape top of sleeve

Keeping chart patt correct throughout, bind off 6 sts at beg of next 2 rows.
Dec 1 st at each end of next 6 rows. 55 sts.
Work even for 22 rows.
Dec 1 st at each end of next 8 rows.
Bind off rem 39 sts.

to finish

Block pieces as explained on page 141.
Sew right shoulder seam, using backstitch.

Neckband

With RS facing and using size 5 (3.75mm) needles and yarn A, pick up and knit 72 sts evenly around front neck edge and 36 sts across back neck edge. 108 sts.
Row 1 (picot row) (WS) P1, *P2tog, yo, rep from * to last st, P1.
Beg with a K row, work 4 rows in St st.
Bind off loosely and evenly.
Sew left shoulder seam and neckband seam.
Fold neckband to WS along picot row and slip stitch loosely in place.
Sew side seams. Sew sleeve seams.
Sew sleeves to armholes, matching center of bound-off edge of sleeve to shoulder seam and easing in fullness at shoulder.
Press seams lightly on WS, following instructions on yarn label and avoiding ribbing.

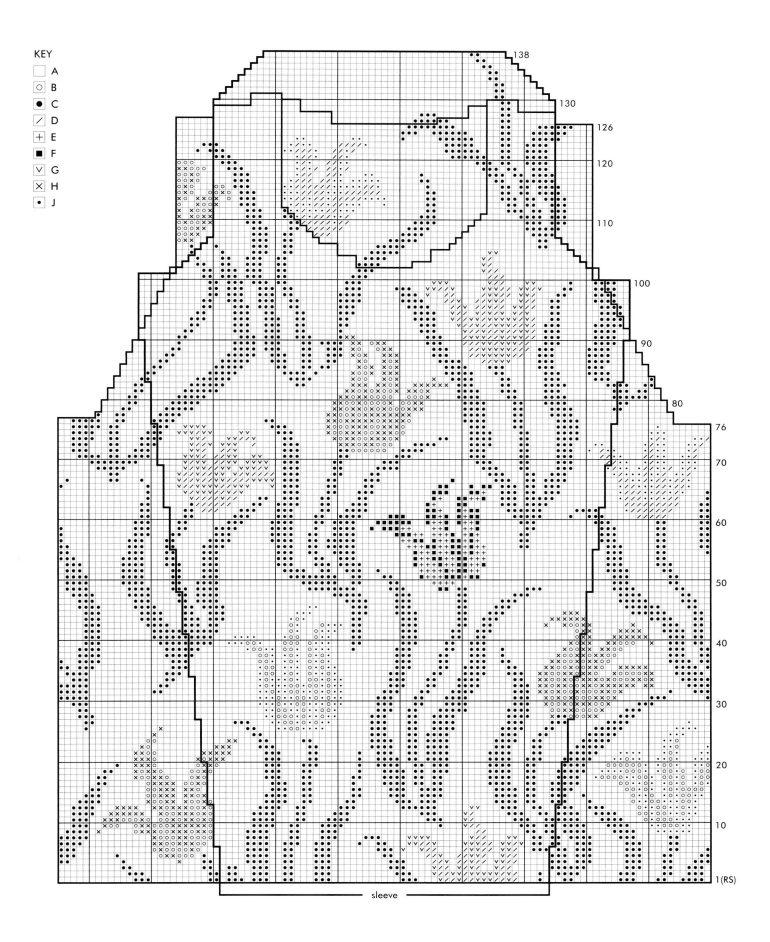

KEY
A
B
C
D
E
F
G
H
J

138
130
126
120
110
100
90
80
76
70
60
50
40
30
20
10
1(RS)

sleeve

gridlock throw

size

Finished throw measures approximately 44in/110cm wide by 57in/142cm tall, including garter st border.

yarn

Rowan *Scottish Tweed 4-Ply* (25g/⅞oz per ball) as foll:

A	Machair 002	1 ball
B	Lewis Grey 007	3 balls
C	Mallard 020	4 balls
D	Celtic Mix 022	12 balls
E	Wine 012	2 balls
F	Heath 014	3 balls
G	Skye 003	2 balls
H	Apple 015	3 balls
J	Winter Navy 021	4 balls
L	Thatch 018	3 balls
M	Midnight 023	3 balls
N	Rust 009	1 ball
Q	Claret 013	2 balls
R	Lavender 005	2 balls
S	Sea Green 006	4 balls
T	Lobster 017	2 balls
U	Peat 019	2 balls
V	Thistle 016	4 balls

needles

Size 8 (5mm) long circular knitting needle, *or size to obtain correct gauge*
Size 7 (4.5mm) long circular needle for border

gauge

20 sts and 25 rows to 4in/10cm measured over St st chart pattern using size 8 (5mm) needles and two strands of yarn. *Note: To save time, take time to check gauge.*

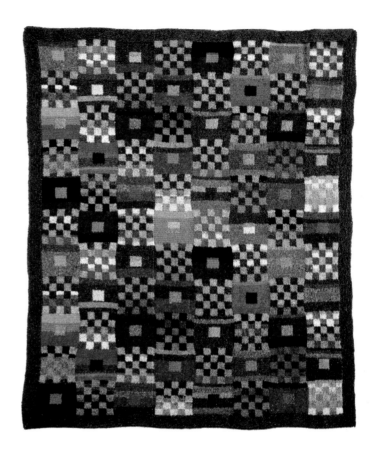

special yarn note

Use two strands of yarn held together throughout.

special chart note

When reading St st chart, read all odd-numbered RS (knit) rows from right to left and all even-numbered WS (purl) rows from left to right. Use a separate length of yarn for each area of color, using the intarsia technique—EXCEPT for individual checkerboard squares. Work across individual checkerboard squares using the Fair Isle technique, weaving color not in use into back of work. Work across small central squares in same way, weaving background yarn on either side of square into back of work. When using the intarsia technique, twist yarns together on WS where they meet to avoid holes.

To avoid weaving in lots of loose ends when knitting is complete, weave in ends on WS of knitting when joining in and cutting off yarns.

to make throw

Using size 7 (4.5mm) circular needle and two strands of yarn D held tog, cast on 216 sts loosely.

Using *two strands of each yarn color* and working back and forth in rows on circular needle throughout, work garter st border as foll:

Row 1 K2tog, K to last 2 sts, K2tog.

Row 2 K to end.

Rep rows 1 and 2 seven times more. 200 sts.

Change to size 8 (5mm) circular needle.

Set St st chart patt (see pages 128 and 129) on next 2 rows as foll:

Chart row 1 (RS) K to end, working [5A, 5B] twice, 5A, 25C, [5D, 5E] twice, 5D, 25F, [5G, 5H] twice, 5G, 25J, [5L, 5M] twice, 5L, 25V.

Chart row 2 (WS) P to end, working 25V, [5L, 5M] twice, 5L, 25J, [5G, 5H] twice, 5G, 25F, [5D, 5E] twice, 5D, 25C, [5A, 5B] twice, 5A.

Cont in St st chart patt as set until chart row 180 has been completed, then work chart rows 1–150 again so that 11 rows of squares in total have been worked, ending with a WS (P) row.

Top border

Change to size 7 (4.5mm) circular needle.

Work garter st border as foll:

Using two strands of yarn D held tog, knit 1 row.

**Working in garter st (knit every row), inc 1 st at each end of next row and then every foll alt row 7 times. 216 sts.

Bind off knitwise.**

to finish

Block knitting as explained on page 141.

Side borders

Work garter st border along each side edge of throw as foll:

With RS facing and using size 7 (4.5mm) circular needle and two strands of yarn D held tog, pick up and knit 275 along side edge of throw (picking up 25 sts along the edge of each large knitted square or 5 sts for every 6 rows).

Complete as for top border from ** to **.

Sew together mitered ends of borders at corners.

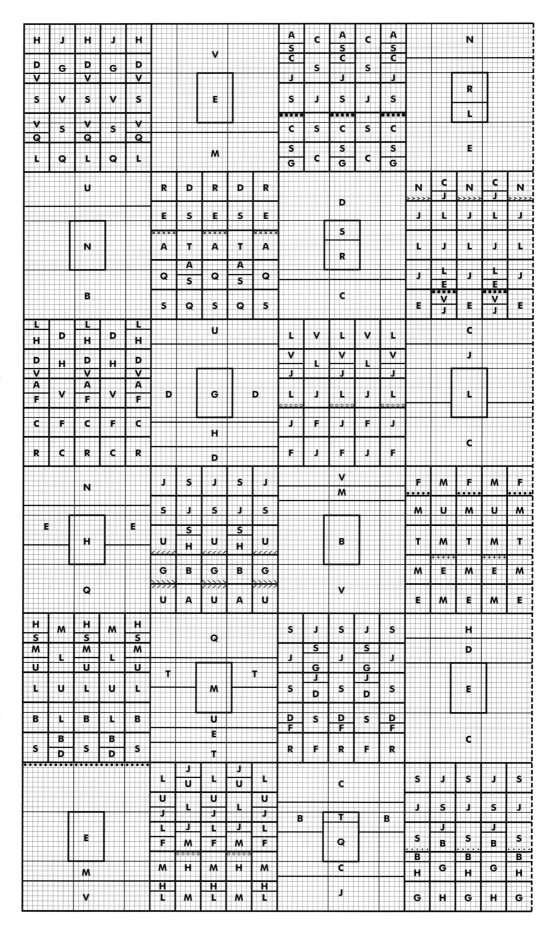

KEY

╲	A
╱	B
═	C
○	F
•	G
│	H
■	J
>	L
∨	N
∧	Q
─	R
✕	S
+	T
●	U

note: The chart is split down the center and positioned across two pages, so be sure to work each row across the entire chart.

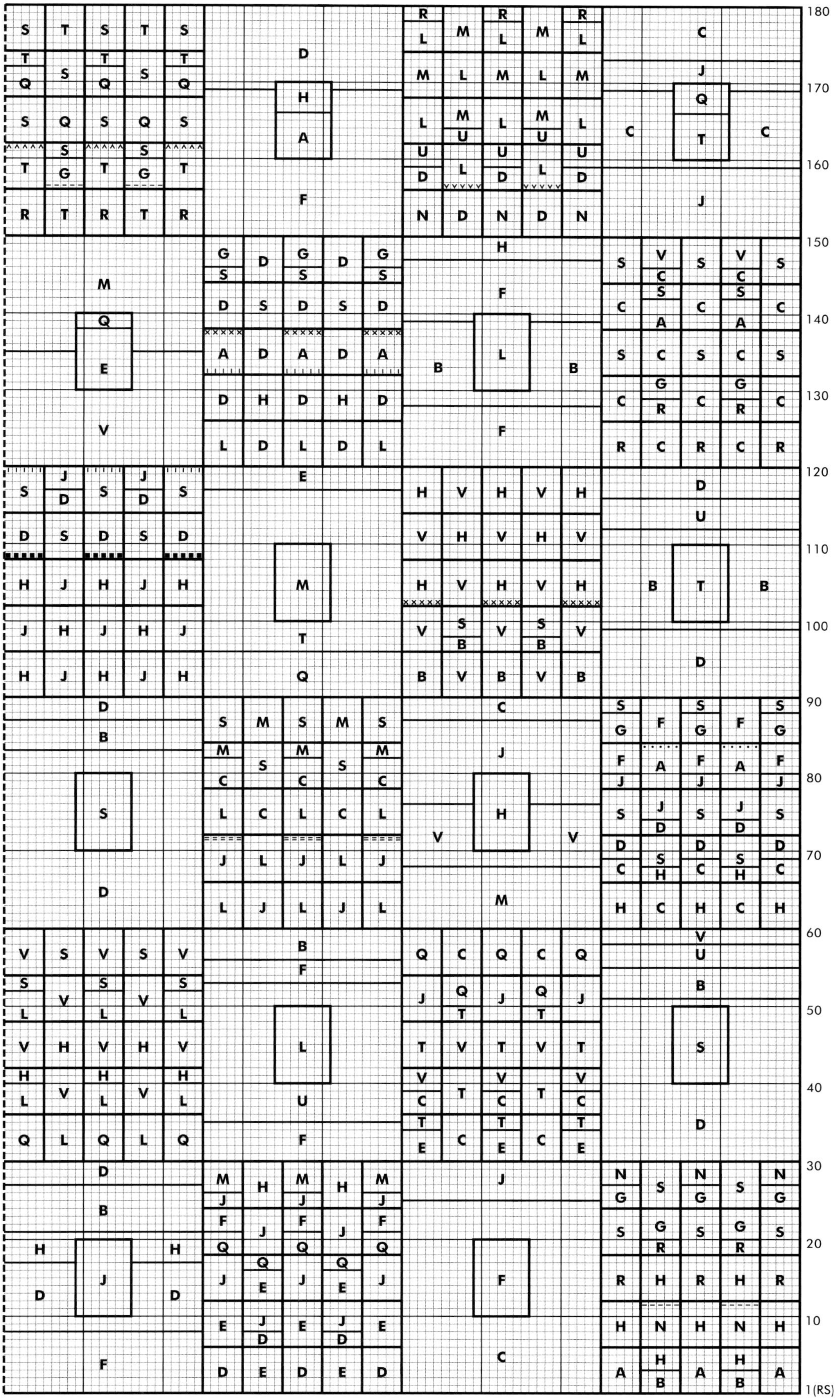
180
170
160
150
140
130
120
110
100
90
80
70
60
50
40
30
20
10
1(RS)

gridlock cushion

size
Finished cushion measures approximately 23¼in/58cm wide by 22½in/56cm tall.

yarn
Rowan *Scottish Tweed 4-Ply* (25g/⅞oz per ball) as foll:

A	Machair 002	1 ball
B	Lewis Grey 007	1 ball
C	Mallard 020	1 ball
D	Celtic Mix 022	1 ball
E	Wine 012	1 ball
F	Heath 014	1 ball
G	Skye 003	1 ball
H	Apple 015	1 ball
J	Winter Navy 021	1 ball
L	Thatch 018	1 ball
M	Midnight 023	1 ball
N	Rust 009	1 ball
Q	Claret 013	1 ball
R	Lavender 005	1 ball
S	Sea Green 006	1 ball
T	Lobster 017	1 ball
U	Peat 019	1 ball
V	Thistle 016	1 ball

needles
Pair of size 6 (4mm) knitting needles, *or size to obtain correct gauge*

extras
Pillow form to fit finished cover
Fabric and matching thread, for backing

gauge
24 sts and 32 rows to 4in/10cm measured over St st chart pattern using size 6 (4mm) needles and one strand of yarn. *Note: To save time, take time to check gauge.*

special chart note
Use the special chart note and chart for the Gridlock Throw (see pages 126, 128, and 129) for this cushion. The chart is used in a slightly amended form for the cushion. Follow the written rows for chart rows 1 and 2 and rows 11 and 12 carefully. You will see that each big square on the cushion is 20 stitches wide rather than 25 stitches wide as on the Gridlock Throw chart; each small checkerboard square is 4 stitches wide rather than 5; and each large center square in the plain squares is only 6 stitches wide rather than 7. Also, there are only 7 big squares across the cushion, unlike the throw which has 8 big squares across its width. (Only one strand of yarn is used for the cushion.)

to make cushion front

Using size 6 (4mm) needles and yarn D, cast on 140 sts.

Foll chart as explained in special chart note on opposite page, set St st chart patt on next 2 rows as foll:

Chart row 1 (RS) K to end, working [4A, 4B] twice, 4A, 20C, [4D, 4E] twice, 4D, 20F, [4G, 4H] twice, 4G, 20J, [4L, 4M] twice, 4L.

Chart row 2 (WS) P to end, working [4L, 4M] twice, 4L, 20J, [4G, 4H] twice, 4G, 20F, [4D, 4E] twice, 4D, 20C, [4A, 4B] twice, 4A.

Keeping width of squares size as set in last 2 rows and foll same number of rows and in colors as on chart, cont in St st chart patt as set until chart row 10 has been completed, then set chart patt on next 2 rows as foll:

Chart row 11 (RS) K to end, working [4H, 4N] twice, 4H, 7C, 6F, 7C, [4E, 4J] twice, 4E, 7D, 6J, 7D, [4B, 4G] twice, 4B, 7C, 6Q, 7C, [4M, 4H] twice, 4M.

Chart row 12 (WS) P to end, working [4M, 4F] twice, 4M, 7C, 6Q, 7C, [4B, 4G] twice, 4B, 7D, 6J, 7D, [4E, 4J] twice, 4E, 7C, 6F, 7C, [4H, 4R] twice, 4H.

Working all squares in widths as set throughout, cont to foll chart for rows and colors until chart row 180 has been completed.

Bind off.

to finish

Block knitting as explained on page 141.

Cut piece of fabric to same size as knitted front, plus ½in/1.5cm extra all around for seam allowances. With RS together, sew backing to knitted front, leaving one side open.

Turn right side out and insert pillow form. Sew opening closed. Alternatively, make backing in two separate pieces to make an "envelope" backing (with the two pieces overlapping by 5–6in/13–15cm at center) so that the pillow form can be removed easily.

foolish virgins scarf

size

Finished scarf measures approximately 12in/29cm wide by 68in/173cm long.

yarn

Rowan *Scottish Tweed 4-Ply* (25g/⅞oz per ball) as foll:

A	Winter Navy 021	1 ball
B	Mallard 020	1 ball
C	Rust 009	1 ball
D	Herring 008	1 ball
E	Thistle 016	1 ball
F	Lobster 017	1 ball
G	Apple 015	1 ball
H	Lewis Grey 007	1 ball
J	Skye 003	1 ball
L	Sea Green 006	1 ball
M	Claret 013	1 ball
N	Celtic Mix 022	1 ball
O	Thatch 018	1 ball
Q	Machair 002	1 ball
R	Sunset 011	1 ball
S	Grey Mist 001	1 ball
T	Lavender 005	1 ball
U	Peat 019	1 ball
V	Heath 014	1 ball
W	Midnight 023	1 ball
X	Wine 012	1 ball
Y	Storm Grey 004	1 ball
Z	Brilliant Pink 010	1 ball

needles

Pair of size 3 (3.25mm) knitting needles, *or size to obtain correct gauge*

gauge

26 sts and 34 rows to 4in/10cm measured over St st chart pattern using size 3 (3.25mm) needles. *Note: To save time, take time to check gauge.*

special chart note

When reading St st charts, read all odd-numbered RS (knit) rows from right to left and all even-numbered WS (purl) rows from left to right. Use the Fair Isle technique for chart 3 and main squares on chart 6, weaving color not in use into back of work. Use the intarsia technique for all other charts, using a separate length of yarn for each area of color and twisting yarns together on WS where they meet to avoid holes.

To avoid weaving in lots of loose ends when knitting is complete, weave in ends on WS of knitting when joining in and cutting off yarns.

to make scarf

Using size 3 (3.25mm) needles and yarn A, cast on 79 sts.
Work border as foll:

Row 1 (RS) P to end.

Row 2 K to end.

Row 3 P to end.

Cut off yarn A.

Row 4 (WS) Using yarn B, P to end.

Row 5 Using yarn B, P to end.

Row 6 Using yarn B, K to end.

Beg with a K row (RS), work rows 1–16 of chart 1 (see page 134), ending with a WS row.

Beg with a K row, work 4 rows in St st in stripes as foll:

1 row A, 1 row H, 1 row J, and 1 row A.

Beg with a K row, work rows 1–89 of chart 2, ending with a RS row.

Using yarn A, P 1 row.

Beg with a K row, work rows 1–3 of chart 3, ending with a RS row.

Using yarn J, P 1 row.

Beg with a K row, work rows 1–13 of chart 4, ending with a RS row.

Using yarn E, P 1 row.

Beg with a K row, work rows 1–37 of chart 5, ending with a RS row.

Using yarn D, P 1 row.

Beg with a K row, work rows 1–7 of chart 6, ending with a RS row.

Using yarn E, P 1 row.

Beg with a K row, work rows 1–88 of chart 7, ending with a WS row.

This completes first half of scarf.

Beg with a K row, rep rows 1–88 of chart 7, ending with a WS row.

Using yarn E and beg with a K row, work 2 rows in St st, ending with a WS row.

For other end of scarf, turn charts upside down and work them in a mirror image as foll:

Turn chart upside down and beg with a K row, work 7 rows of chart 6, ending with a RS row.

Using yarn D, P 1 row.

Turn chart upside down and beg with a K row, work 37 rows of chart 5, ending with a RS row.

Using yarn E, P 1 row.

Turn chart upside down and beg with a K row, work 13 rows of chart 4, ending with a RS row.

Using yarn J, P 1 row.

Turn chart upside down and beg with a K row, work 3 rows of chart 3, ending with a RS row.

Using yarn A, P 1 row.

Turn chart upside down and beg with a K row, work 89 rows of chart 2, ending with a RS row.

Beg with a P row, work 5 rows in St st in stripes as foll:

1 row A, 1 row J, 1 row H, and 2 rows A.

Turn chart upside down and beg with a K row, work 16 rows of chart 1, ending with a WS row.

Work border as foll:

Next row (RS) Using yarn B, P to end.

Next row Using yarn B, K to end.

Next row Using yarn B, P to end.

Cut off yarn B.

Next row (WS) Using yarn A, P to end.

Next row Using yarn A, P to end.

Next row Using yarn A, K to end.

Using yarn A, bind off purlwise.

to finish

Weave in any rem loose ends.
Block scarf as explained on page 141.

KEY

- ■ A
- + B
- − C
- ✕ E
- ○ F
- < G
- ‖ J
- > L
- ∧ M
- ● N
- | O
- ＼ Q
- · S
- ⁄ T
- ＝ Z

note: The detail of the scarf on the opposite page shows the top end of the scarf, so the colors on the tumbling blocks (chart 7) appear reversed.

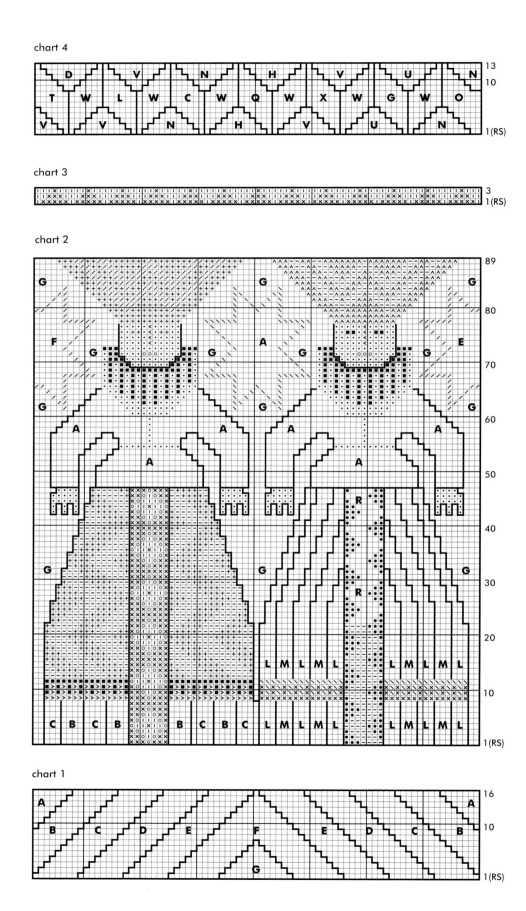

chart 7

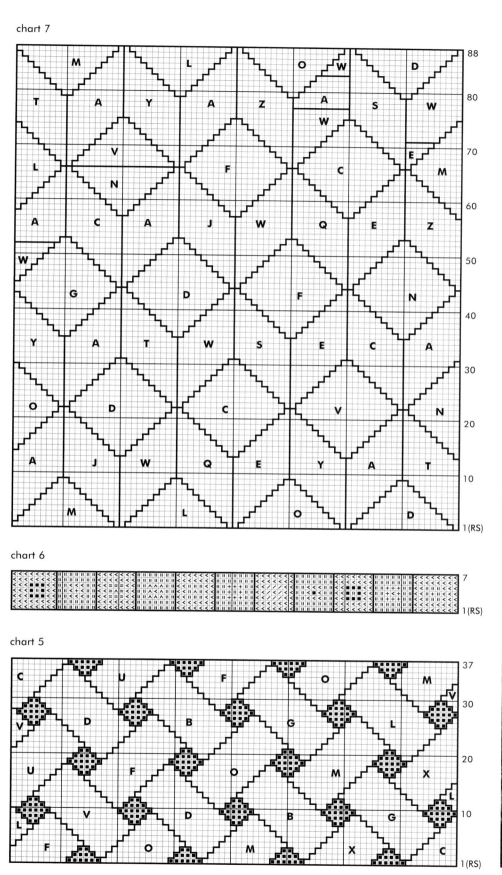

chart 6

chart 5

puzzle

sizes and measurements

To fit bust				
	32–34	36	38–40	in
	81–86	91	97–102	cm

Finished knitted measurements

Around bust	40	42	44	in
	102	107	112	cm
Length to shoulder	20½	21½	22½	in
	52	54.5	57	cm
Sleeve seam	19	19	19	in
	48.5	48.5	48.5	cm

yarn

Rowan *Scottish Tweed 4-Ply* (25g/⅞oz per ball) as foll:

A	Winter Navy 021	10	11	12	balls
B	Herring 008	7	7	7	balls
C	Sea Green 006	1	1	1	ball
D	Claret 013	1	1	1	ball
E	Wine 012	1	1	1	ball
F	Apple 015	1	1	1	ball
G	Rust 009	1	1	1	ball

needles

Pair of size 2 (2.75mm) knitting needles
Pair of size 3 (3.25mm) knitting needles, *or size to obtain correct gauge*

extras

7 buttons

gauge

29 sts and 32 rows to 4in/10cm measured over St st chart pattern using size 3 (3.25mm) needles. *Note: To save time, take time to check gauge.*

special chart note

When reading St st charts, read all odd-numbered RS (knit) rows from right to left and all even-numbered WS (purl) rows from left to right. Use the Fair Isle technique for background and grid (yarns A and B), weaving colors not in use into back of work. Use the intarsia technique for contrasting squares, using a separate length of yarn for each area of color and twisting yarns together on WS where they meet to avoid holes.

To avoid weaving in lots of loose ends when knitting is complete, weave in ends on WS of knitting when joining in and cutting off yarns.

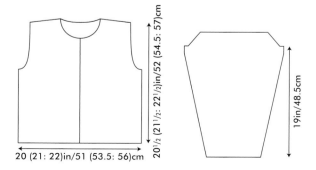

20½ (21½: 22½)in/52 (54.5: 57)cm

20 (21: 22)in/51 (53.5: 56)cm

19in/48.5cm

back

Using size 2 (2.75mm) needles and yarn B, cast on 147 (155: 163) sts.
Work garter st border in stripes as foll:
Row 1 (RS) Using yarn A, K to end.
Row 2 Rep row 1.
Row 3 Using yarn B, K to end.
Row 4 Rep row 3.
Rows 5–12 Rep rows 1–4 twice.
Change to size 3 (3.25mm) needles.
Using yarn A, K 1 row (chart row 1).

Set St st chart patt (see pages 138 and 139) on next 2 rows as foll:

Chart row 2 (WS) P across row, working 4 (8: 12)A, 1B, 5A, [25B, 5A] 4 times, 17 (21: 25)B.

Chart row 3 K across row, working 4 (8: 12)A, *1B, 5A, 1B, 5D, 1B, 5A, 1B, 11A, 1B, 5A, 1B, 5E, 1B, 5A, 1B,* 11A, 1B, 5A, 1B, 5F, 1B, 5A, 1B, 11A, rep from * to * once, 4 (8: 12)A.
Working between markers for back for chosen size, cont as set until chart row 90 (98: 106) has been completed, ending with a WS row.

Shape armholes

Keeping chart patt correct throughout, bind off 4 sts at beg of next 2 rows.

Dec 1 st at each end of next 5 rows and 5 foll alt rows. 119 (127: 135) sts.

Work even until chart row 154 (162: 170) has been completed, ending with a WS row.

Shape shoulders and back neck

Bind off 12 (14: 15) sts at beg of next 2 rows.

Next row (RS) Bind off 13 (14: 15) sts, work in patt until there are 17 (19: 20) sts on right needle, then turn, leaving rem sts on a holder.

Cont on these 17 (19: 20) sts only for right side of neck.

Bind off 4 sts at beg of next row.

Bind off rem 13 (14: 16) sts.

With RS facing, rejoin yarn to rem sts and bind off center 35 sts, then work in patt to end.

Complete to match first side, reversing shapings.

pocket linings (make 2)

Using size 3 (3.25mm) needles and yarn A, cast on 34 sts.
Beg with a K row, work 32 (34: 36) rows in St st, ending with a WS row.

Leave sts on a holder.

left front

Using size 2 (2.75mm) needles and yarn B, cast on 80 (84: 88) sts.

Work garter st border in stripes as foll:

Row 1 (RS) Using yarn A, K to end.

Row 2 Rep row 1.

Row 3 Using yarn B, K to end.

Row 4 Rep row 3.

Rows 5–8 Rep rows 1–4.

Rows 9–11 Rep rows 1–3.

Row 12 (WS) Using yarn B, K6 and leave these sts on a holder for front band, K to end. 74 (78: 82) sts.

Change to size 3 (3.25mm) needles.

Beg color patt from chart row 1 and working between markers for left front, work until chart row 32 (34: 36) has been completed, ending with a WS row.

Place pocket lining

Chart row 31 (RS) Work first 18 (20: 22) sts in patt, slip next 34 sts onto a holder and work in patt across 34 sts of first pocket lining, work rem sts in patt.

Cont in chart patt until chart row 90 (98: 106) has been completed, ending with a WS row.

Shape armhole

Keeping chart patt correct throughout, bind off 4 sts at beg of next row.

Work even for 1 row.

Dec 1 st at armhole edge on next 5 rows and 5 foll alt rows. 60 (64: 68) sts.

Work even until chart row 131 (139: 147) has been completed, ending at neck edge.

Shape front neck

Bind off 9 sts at beg of next row and 4 sts at beg of foll alt row.

Dec 1 st at neck edge on next 4 rows, 4 foll alt rows and 1 foll 4th row. 38 (42: 46) sts.

Work even until chart row 154 (162: 170) has been completed, ending with a WS row.

Shape shoulder

Bind off 12 (14: 15) sts at beg of next row.

Work even for 1 row.

Bind off 13 (14: 15) sts at beg of next row.

Work even for 1 row.

Bind off rem 13 (14: 16) sts.

right front

Using size 2 (2.75mm) needles and yarn B, cast on 80 (84: 88) sts.

Work garter st border in stripes as foll:

Row 1 (RS) Using yarn A, K to end.

Row 2 Rep row 1.

Row 3 Using yarn B, K to end.

Row 4 Rep row 3.

Rows 5 and 6 Rep row 1.

Row 7 (buttonhole row) (RS) Using yarn B, K2, yo, K2tog, K to end.

Row 8 Rep row 3.

Rows 9 and 10 Rep row 1.

Rows 11 Rep row 3.

Row 12 (WS) Using yarn B, K to last 6 sts, then turn, leaving last 6 sts on a holder for front band. 74 (78: 82) sts.

Change to size 3 (3.25mm) needles.

Complete as for left front, but following chart between markers for right front and reversing shapings and pocket placement.

sleeves (make 2)

Using size 2 (2.75mm) needles and yarn B, cast on 67 sts.

Work 12 rows in garter st stripe as for back.

Change to size 3 (3.25mm) needles.

Beg with sleeve chart row 1 (see page 140), work in chart patt *and at the same time* inc 1 st at each end of 3rd row, 6 foll 4th rows, and then every foll 6th row until there are 117 sts.

Work even until chart row 144 has been completed, ending with a WS row.

Shape top of sleeve

Keeping chart patt correct throughout, bind off 4 sts at beg of next 2 rows.

Dec 1 st at each end of next row and 4 foll alt rows. 99 sts.

Dec 1 st at each end of every row until 85 sts rem.

Bind off loosely and evenly.

to finish

Block pieces as explained on page 141.

Sew both shoulder seams, using backstitch.

Button band

With RS facing, using size 2 (2.75mm) needles and keeping stripe sequence correct, cont in garter st until band (when slightly stretched) fits neatly up front edge to beg of neck shaping.

Slip stitch band in place, then bind off.

Mark positions of 7 buttons, the first to correspond with buttonhole on right front, the last ½in/1cm below neck edge, and the rem 5 evenly spaced between.

Buttonhole band

Work buttonhole band to match button band, working buttonholes to match positions of button markers as foll:

Buttonhole row (RS) K2, yo, K2tog, K2.

Pocket tops

With RS facing and using size 2 (2.75mm) needles and yarn B, K across 34 sts on holder for first pocket top.

Work 8 rows in garter st in stripes as foll:

1 row B, 2 rows A, 2 rows B, 2 rows A, 1 row B.

Using yarn B, bind off knitwise.

Work second pocket top in same way.

Collar

Using size 2 (2.75mm) needles and yarn B, cast on 20 sts.

Work in garter st stripe as for back until collar measures 18in/46cm from cast-on edge, ending with 1 row of yarn B.

Using yarn B, bind off neatly knitwise on WS.

Positioning ends of collar halfway across front bands and matching center of collar with center back neck, slip stitch collar neatly to neck edge.

Sew side seams and sleeve seams.

Sew sleeves to armholes, matching center of bound-off edge of sleeve to shoulder seam.

Press seams lightly on WS, following instructions on yarn label and avoiding garter st.

Sew on buttons to correspond with buttonholes.

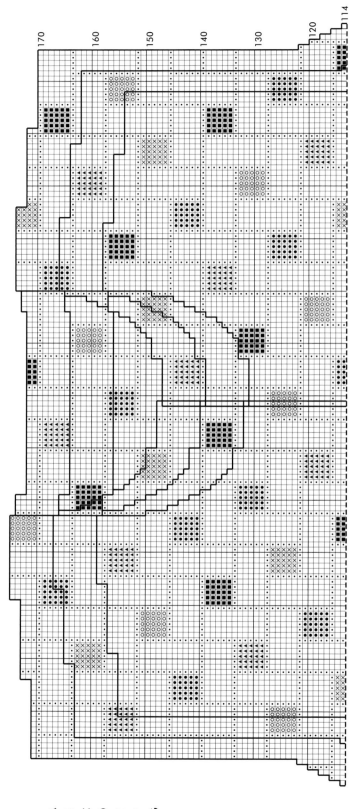

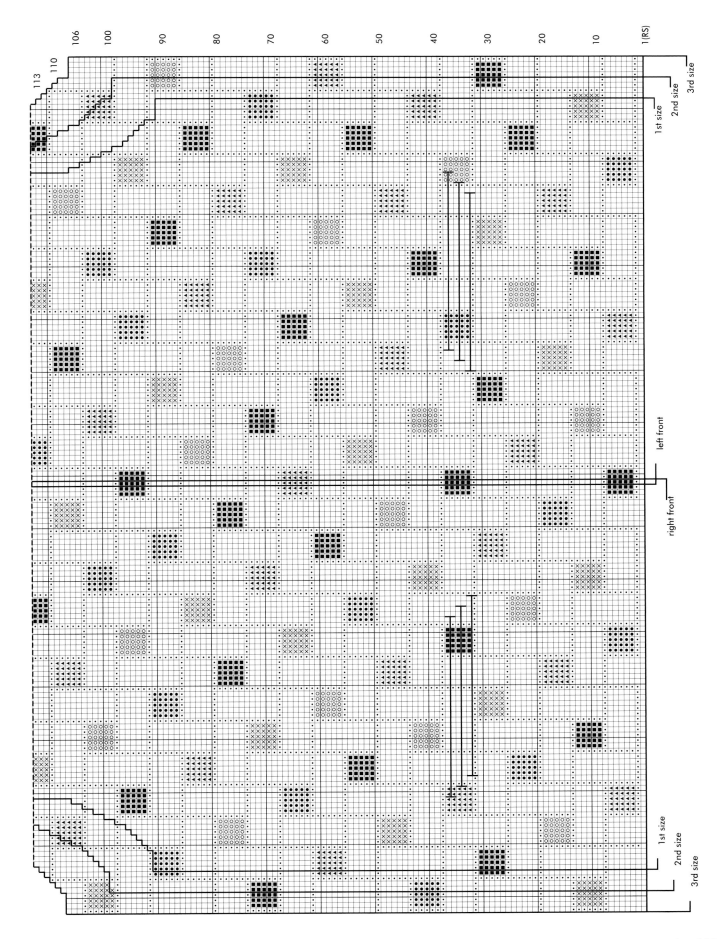

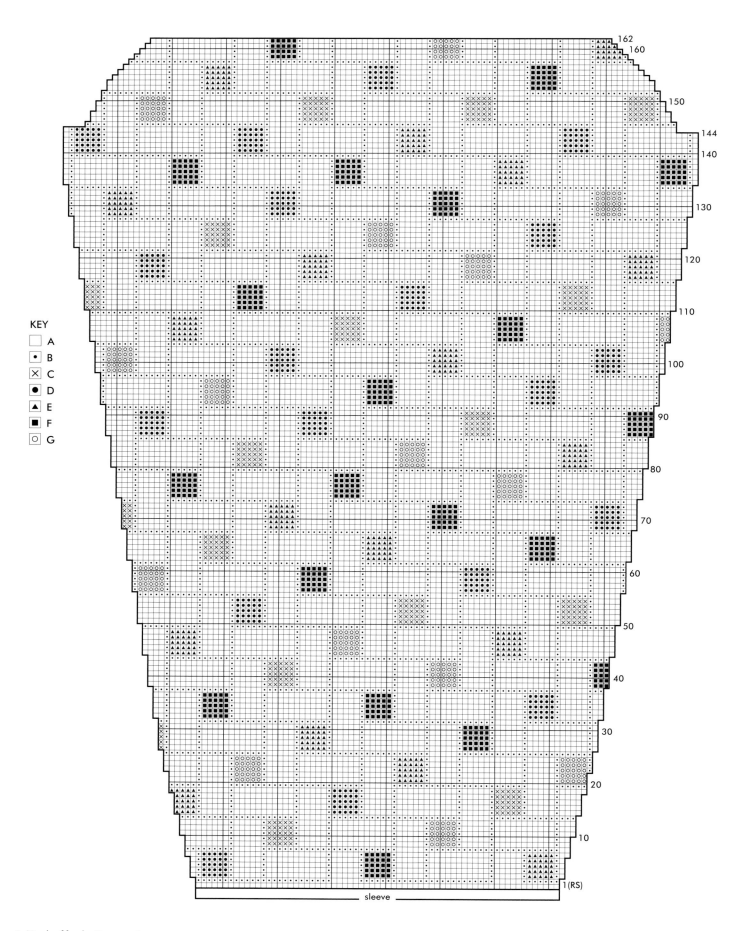

KEY

A
B ·
C ×
D ●
E ▲
F ■
G ○

162
160
150
144
140
130
120
110
100
90
80
70
60
50
40
30
20
10
1(RS)

sleeve

knitting know-how

Here are some knitting technique tips to help you achieve a successful finished knit.

gauge

Obtaining the correct gauge can make the difference between a successful garment and a disastrous one. It controls both the shape and size of the knitting, so any variation, however slight, can distort the finished garment.

The gauge that you must match is given at the start of each pattern. To check your gauge, knit a square in the pattern stitch of 5–10 more stitches and 5–10 more rows than those given in the gauge note. Press the finished square under a damp cloth and mark out the central 4in/10cm square with pins. If you have too many stitches to 4in/10cm, try again using thicker needles. If you have too few stitches to 4in/10cm, try again using finer needles. Once you have achieved the correct gauge, your garment will be knitted to the measurements shown in the size diagram with the pattern.

sizing and size diagrams

The instructions are given for the smallest size, and larger sizes follow in parentheses. If there is only one set of figures, it refers to all sizes. If - (hyphen) or 0 (zero) is given in an instruction for the size you are knitting, then that particular instruction does not apply to your size.

Included with the garments in this book is a size diagram of the finished pieces and their dimensions. The size diagram shows the finished width of the garment at the underarm, and it is this measurement that you should choose first; a useful tip is to measure one of your own garments that is a comfortable fit. Having chosen a size based on width, look at the corresponding length for that size; if you are not happy with the total recommended length, adjust your own garment before beginning your armhole shaping—any adjustment after this point will mean that your sleeve will not fit into your garment easily. Don't forget to take your adjustment into account if there is any side-seam shaping.

Finally, look at the sleeve length; the size diagram shows the finished sleeve measurement, taking into account any top-arm insertion length. Measure your body between the center of your neck and your wrist; this measurement should correspond to half the garment width plus the sleeve length. Again, your sleeve length may be adjusted, but remember to take into consideration your sleeve increases if you do adjust the length—you must increase more frequently than the pattern states to shorten your sleeve, less frequently to lengthen it.

knitting charts

Most of the patterns in the book are worked from a chart. Each square on a chart represents a stitch and each line of squares a row of knitting. Each color used is given a different symbol or letter and these are shown near the beginning of the pattern, or in the key alongside the chart of each pattern. When working from the charts, read odd rows (knit) from right to left and even rows (purl) from left to right, unless otherwise stated.

colorwork knitting

There are two main methods of working color into a knitted fabric—the intarsia and Fair Isle techniques. The first method produces a single thickness of fabric and is generally used where a color is only required in a particular area of a row and does not form a repeating pattern across the row, as in the Fair Isle technique.

Intarsia color knitting: Cut short lengths of yarn for each motif or block of color used in a row. Then, joining in the various colors at the appropriate point on the row, link one color to the next by twisting them around each other where they meet on the wrong side to avoid gaps. All yarn ends can then either be darned along the color join lines as each motif is completed, or they can be knitted into the fabric of the knitting as each color is worked into the pattern. This is done in much the same way as "weaving in" yarns when working the Fair Isle technique and saves time. It is essential that the gauge is noted for intarsia as this may vary from the stockinette stitch if both are used in the same pattern.

Fair Isle color knitting: When two or three colors are worked repeatedly across a row, strand the yarn not in use loosely behind the stitches being worked. If you are working with more than two colors, treat the floating yarns as if they were one yarn and always spread the stitches to their correct width to keep them elastic. It is advisable not to carry the stranded or floating yarns over more than three stitches at a time, but to weave them under and over the color you are working. This catches the floating yarns into the back (wrong side) of the work.

finishing instructions

After working for hours on your knitting, it is worthwhile finishing it with care. Follow the tips below for a truly professional-looking garment.

Blocking and pressing: Before blocking and pressing, darn in all ends neatly along the selvage edge or a color join, as appropriate. Be sure to refer to the yarn label for pressing instructions before ironing.

Block out each piece of knitting using pins and gently press each piece (avoiding the ribbing and garter stitch), using a warm iron over a damp cloth. Take special care to press the edges, as this will make sewing seams both easier and neater.

Sewing pieces together: When sewing the knitted pieces together, remember to match areas of color and texture very carefully where they meet. Use a seam stitch such as backstitch or mattress stitch for all main knitting seams and join all ribbing and neckbands with a flat seam, unless otherwise stated.

Having completed the pattern instructions, sew the seams in the order instructed. Slip stitch any pocket edgings and pocket linings in place. After all the seams are complete, press the seams and hems.

Lastly, sew on the buttons to correspond with the positions of the buttonholes.

knitting abbreviations

The abbreviations below are those used in the knitting patterns in this book. (Any special abbreviations are given within the individual patterns.)

alt	alternate
beg	begin(ning)
cm	centimeter(s)
cont	continu(e)(ing)
dec	decreas(e)(ing)
DK	double knitting (a medium-weight yarn)
foll	follow(s)(ing)
g	gram(s)
in	inch(es)
inc	increas(e)(ing); increase one st by working into front and back of st
K	knit
K2tog	knit next 2 sts together
m	meter(s)
M1	make one stitch by picking up loop between last and next st and working into the back of this loop
mm	millimeter(s)
oz	ounce(s)
P	purl
P2tog	purl next 2 sts together
patt	pattern; or work in pattern
rem	remain(s)(ing)
rev St st	reverse stockinette st; purl RS rows and knit WS rows
rep	repeat(s)(ing)
RS	right side
sl	slip
st(s)	stitch(es)
St st	stockinette stitch; knit RS rows and purl WS rows
tbl	through back of loop(s)
tog	together
WS	wrong side
yd	yard(s)
yo	yarn over right needle to make an extra stitch

* Repeat instructions after asterisk or between asterisks as many times as instructed.

[ ] Repeat instructions inside brackets as many times as instructed.

yarn information

The following are the specifications of the Rowan yarns used for the designs in this book. It is always best to try to obtain the exact yarns specified in the patterns. If, however, you wish to find a substitute yarn, use the yarn descriptions given below to find a similar yarn type and weight. When substituting yarn, always remember to calculate the yarn amount needed by yardage rather than by ball weight.

For yarn care directions, refer to the yarn label.

Rowan Cotton Glace
A fine-weight cotton yarn; 100 percent cotton; 50g/1¾oz (approximately 126yd/115m) per ball; recommended gauge—23 sts and 32 rows to 4in/10cm measured over St st using sizes 3–5 (3.25–3.75mm) knitting needles.

Rowan 4-Ply Cotton
A super-fine-weight cotton yarn; 100 percent cotton; 50g/1¾oz (approximately 186yd/170m) per ball; recommended gauge—27–29 sts and 37–39 rows to 4in/10cm measured over St st using sizes 2–3 (2.75–3.25mm) knitting needles.

Rowan Handknit Cotton
A medium-weight cotton yarn; 100 percent cotton; 50g/1¾oz (approximately 93yd/85m) per ball; recommended gauge—19–20 sts and 28 rows to 4in/10cm measured over St st using sizes 6–7 (4–4.5mm) knitting needles.

Rowan Scottish Tweed 4-Ply
A fine-weight wool yarn; 100 percent pure new wool; 25g/⅞oz (approximately 120yd/110m) per ball; recommended gauge—26–28 sts and 38–40 rows to 4in/10cm measured over St st using sizes 2–3 (2.75–3.25mm) knitting needles.

Rowan Scottish Tweed DK
A lightweight wool yarn; 100 percent pure new wool; 50g/1¾oz (approximately 123yd/113m) per ball; recommended gauge—20–22 sts and 28–30 rows to 4in/10cm measured over St st using size 6 (4mm) knitting needles.

Rowan Scottish Tweed Chunky
A bulky-weight wool yarn; 100 percent pure new wool; 100g/3½oz (approximately 109yd/100m) per ball; recommended gauge—12 sts and 16 rows to 4in/10cm measured over St st using size 11 (8mm) knitting needles.

Rowan Summer Tweed
A medium-weight silk/cotton blend yarn; 70 percent silk and 30 percent cotton; 50g/1¾oz (approximately 118yd/108m) per hank; recommended gauge—16 sts and 23 rows to 4in/10cm measured over St st using size 8 (5mm) knitting needles.

yarn suppliers

Rowan yarns are widely distributed. To find a yarn store near you, contact Westminster Fibers Inc. (see below) or visit the Rowan website at www.knitrowan.com, which also has a list of online suppliers.

Westminster Fibers Inc., 165 Ledge Street, Nashua, New Hampshire 03060.
Tel: 1 (603) 886 5041/5043.
Fax: 1 (603) 886 1056.
E-mail: rowan@westminsterfibers.com

Craft Yarn Council of America's Standard Yarn Weight System

Categories of yarn, gauge ranges, and recommended needle sizes

Yarn Weight Symbol & Category Names	1 SUPER FINE	2 FINE	3 LIGHT	4 MEDIUM	5 BULKY	6 SUPER BULKY
Type of Yarns in Category	Sock, Fingering, Baby	Sport, Baby	DK, Light Worsted	Worsted, Afghan, Aran	Chunky, Craft, Rug	Bulky, Roving
Knit Gauge Range* in Stockinette Stitch to 4 inches	27–32 sts	23–26 sts	21–24 sts	16–20 sts	12–15 sts	6–11 sts
Recommended Needle in Metric Size Range	2.25–3.25 mm	3.25–3.75 mm	3.75–4.5 mm	4.5–5.5 mm	5.5–8 mm	8mm and larger
Recommended Needle U.S. Size Range	1 to 3	3 to 5	5 to 7	7 to 9	9 to 11	9 to 11

*__Guidelines only:__ The above reflect the most commonly used gauges and needle sizes for specific yarn categories.

author's acknowledgments

I want to thank my trusty and talented knitters—Wendy Harvey, Kyoko Nakayoshi, Jenny Shore, Michelle Tive-Hive, Eva Yates, Juliana Yeo—for their efforts and meeting the deadlines. Revisiting this collection of knit designs from the past has been a really enjoyable experience. Working with three highly professional publishing colleagues—Sally Harding, who organized the knitting and edited this book, Christine Wood, who laid out the book with her usual great style, and Susan Berry, who conceived it and oversaw each detail. There was a real party atmosphere at our shoots—as those of us who were recording the knitwear on the film gathered at the wonderful Charleston House. Hair and make-up artist Joanna Bernacka did her magic. Models Marzena Pokrzywnska, Robin Scott, Mak Gilchrist, Dan Carver, and Belinda Mably did their job spontaneously, and Elaine Briggs styled the shots with imagination. Sheila Rock and her brilliant, hard-working assistant, Kevin Curtis, worked tirelessly, making the knitwear glow in the amazing setting of Charleston. And the crew at Charleston House were helpful and appreciative of our work, which made everything go smoothly.

Thanks to Yvonne Mably for feeding and housing us so graciously, and the biggest thanks to Brandon Mably for his neverending attention to detail for the months of birth pains on this book.

Note: Rowan Yarns are grateful to Charleston House for their permission to photograph at such a historic location. For those wishing to visit Charleston themselves, please check their website, www.charleston.org.uk, for details.